Chi:
Life Hacks
For Girls*

How to Hack Life's Secret Code to Health, Happiness and Success That Lies Deep Within Us All

Dr Chi, Rita Pei Lee

*Disclaimer: For editorial clarity and simplicity, I have used the terms "girls" and "young women" when I am referring to any person that identifies as Agender, Androgynous, Bigender, Cisgender, Demigirl, Female, Gender-Creative, Gender-Diverse, Gender-Expansive, Gender-Fluid, Genderless, Gender-Nonconforming, Gender-Questioning, Neutrois, Nonbinary, Pangender, Polygender, Third Gender, Two-Spirit, X-Gender and many others. I personally identify as Genderless, so no offence was intended in my attempt to include all of us. If anyone is offended, I sincerely apologise.

Chi: Life Hacks for Girls* © copyright 2024 by Rita Pei Lee. All rights reserved.
No part of this book may be reproduced in any form whatsoever, by photography, or xerography or by any other means, by broadcast or transmission, by translation into any kind of language, nor by recording electronically or otherwise, without permission in writing from the author, except by a reviewer, who may quote brief passages in critical articles or reviews.

ISBN: 9798884744332

First published in Great Britain by TurnerFraise Publishing

This book is dedicated to the millions of girls and young women around the world who sometimes doubt themselves, don't always want to speak up, or don't know how to unlock their full potential.

Never stop dreaming, we got this.

Stay Strong
Dr Chi

CONTENTS

FOREWORD by Catarina Pereira, Founder of HotChi

INTRODUCTION

CHAPTER 1: INTRODUCTION TO CHI
Conceptual Overview of Chi 2
Historical Roots of Chi 4
Modern Interpretations of Chi 6
Importance of Chi in Personal Development 10

CHAPTER 2: FOUNDATIONS OF CHI
Philosophical Underpinnings of Chi 16
Traditional Chinese Medicine and Chi 18
Scientific Perspectives on Chi 21
Cultural Significance of Chi 24

CHAPTER 3: NAVIGATING MENTAL WELLBEING
The Impact of Mental Health on Emotional Wellbeing 27
The Growing Mental Health Crisis Among Young Women 29
Societal Expectations and Their Impact on Mental Health 31
Addressing Loneliness, Social Media, and Peer Relationship 33
Empowering Young Women to Prioritise Their Mental Health 36
Why Mindcare Matters: Nurturing Your Inner Beauty 38

CHAPTER 4: PRACTICAL APPLICATIONS OF CHI
Daily Practices for Cultivating Chi 42
Chi in Physical Exercise and Movement 44
Integrating Chi into Work and Daily Life 46
Chi in Relationships and Social Interactions 49

CHAPTER 5: THE SCIENCE BEHIND Aromatherapy
The Limbic System and Emotional Response 53
Neurotransmitters and Brain Chemistry................................56
Essential Oils and Their Therapeutic Properties 58

CHAPTER 6: BREATHWORK AND CHI ACTIVATION
The Role of Breath in Chi Activation......................................65
Techniques for Conscious Breathing......................................67
Breathwork Practices for Energy and Relaxation 68
Breathwork for Emotional Balance and Mental Clarity 71

CHAPTER 7: ACUPRESSURE AND MERIDIANS
Understanding Chi Meridians and Energy Channels 77
Self Acupressure Points for Balancing Chi.............................78
Integrating Acupressure into Daily Self-Care Routines.........81

CHAPTER 8: MEDITATION AND INNER HARMONY
Introduction to Meditation for Chi Cultivation 85
Mindfulness Meditation Practices 86
Meditation Techniques for Connecting with Inner Strength 90

CHAPTER 9: SELF-CARE AND CHI RITUALS
Chi-Infused Beauty and Skincare Rituals...............................95
Aromatherapy for Chi Balance 98
Facial Massage Techniques for Chi Activation.......................98
Creating Personalised Chi Rituals for Self-Care 102

CHAPTER 10: EMPOWERING CONFIDENCE WITH CHI
Building Confidence through Chi Practices 106
Chi Techniques for Overcoming Self-Doubt 108
Cultivating Self-Compassion and Positive Self-Talk with Chi 109
Using Chi to Enhance Assertiveness and Presence..............111

CHAPTER 11: THE SCIENCE OF SEXUAL WELLNESS
Confidence and Self-Affirmation 114
Sensory Sensations and Aromatherapy 115
Inner Beauty and Self-Love 116
Relaxation Techniques and Sensual Bliss...118

CHAPTER 12: INTEGRATING CHI INTO DAILY LIFE
Chi in Everyday Activities and Routines..122
Creating Chi-Inspired Living Spaces 124
Mindful Eating and Nutrition for Chi Balance 126
Chi Practices for Enhancing Sleep and Rest..129

CHAPTER 13: NATURE AND ENVIRONMENTAL HARMONY
Connecting with Nature's Chi 133
Practices for Grounding and Earth Energy 136
Forest Bathing and Chi Healing..137
Environmental Awareness and Chi Preservation......................................138

CHAPTER 14: COMMUNITY AND COLLECTIVE CHI
Creating Chi Communities and Support Networks.....................................141
Chi Circles and Group Practices 142
Collaborative Chi Projects for Social Impact......................................143
Collective Healing and Empowerment through Chi 145

CHAPTER 15: PERSONAL STORIES OF CHI TRANSFORMATION
Chi Journeys of Personal Growth and Transformation........................149
Testimonials of Chi Practices in Daily Life.......................................151
Authentic Stories of Chi Empowerment and Resilience......................154

FINAL THOUGHTS 165

GLOSSARY 167

FOREWORD
by Catarina Pereira, Founder of HotChi

Rita Pei Lee is a pioneer. One of the world's first people to identify as genderless from so far back I wasn't even born; a trail-blazer in the study and application of human psychology; advisor to countless global brands and governments; and dedicated guardian to thousands of vulnerable young women around the world through their tireless work promoting emotional and mental wellbeing through the power of Chi (pronounced "chee").

I'm proud to say Rita—or Dr Chi as they're rightly known—is also my friend and business associate. When I started HotChi, the first mood-boosting *inner* beauty brand, I named my first product **Hack The System** as that's one of the earliest lessons I learned from Dr Chi.

Learning how to hack our emotional and mental wellbeing is the greatest secret to unlocking our true potential. Our brains are amazing but like any highly sophisticated super computer, they can malfunction and crash. Knowing how to reboot your brain is really important, and to continue the computer analogy, we need to make sure any crash is followed by a safe recovery of data. This is the essence of Chi—the balance of our internal life force.

So many young people, particularly young women—the focus of Dr Chi's work—now suffer from emotional mental health issues and don't really know it.

As young women, we often think our emotional glitches are hormonal. Maybe they are, but that often means we dismiss any malfunctions as just part of being a woman. Let me tell you: ***You do not have to put up with stress, anxiety or self-doubt anymore.***

I remember the years from my teens to my early 20s (I'm 27 now) as being particularly confusing for my emotions. It's the time in our lives when we experience profound changes in our state of mind. It's when we develop our ambitions and consider our future. It also happens to coincide with a whole bunch of big decisions we suddenly have to deal with, around love, relationships, education, career choice and financial responsibility (40-year mortgages? Urgh). In short, we have to become adults and if you're like me at the time, I didn't want to be an adult yet.

Working with Dr Chi has been a game-changer for me and my team at HotChi. 35 years and counting of their insights and knowledge have gone into developing our products and sharing our beliefs.

I'm a hustler so I accept that this may look like a flagrant plug for our brand, but it's not. Our brand is the method we use to introduce Chi to a new audience of ambitious teen girls and young women. HotChi's mission—fully endorsed by Dr Chi—is to empower young women to be their best. And giving you the products and knowledge to help you overcome barriers and achieve your dreams is our top priority. We want to live in a world where women and girls develop into world-class leaders, fearless entrepreneurs, business pioneers and wonderful, happy, balanced people in control of everything in their life.

And we prefer prevention over cure. Often with emotional mental issues, needing to find a cure means our condition has already developed. Whilst Chi balance is a remarkable, scientifically proven way to self-correct, it takes time, dedication and patience. I urge you to protect your mental health right now. Think of it like our weight. Once we become overweight to the point it is detrimental to our health, we have to work so much harder to lose it. It can be done, as we all know, but it's tough (not gonna lie).

It's much safer to understand that emotional and mental issues are part of modern life, and to keep on top of our health—physical, emotional and mental—is the recommended medical advice we should follow.

Dr Chi has literally written the book on Chi and emotional mental wellbeing. ***Chi: Life Hacks for Girls**** should be your most prized possession. It's your roadmap to unlocking your potential and nurturing your Chi. The years of advice I was lucky enough to receive from Dr Chi are squeezed into this book, along with so much more. Read it cover to cover, absorb it, believe it, learn from it and you'll get to live your best life.

Catarina Pereira
London

INTRODUCTION

I grew up on Hong Kong Island in the 1970s and 80s. Back then, it was a very different place to what it is now, though the signs from the past are still there if you know where to look. I love the energy and the culture today but back then, Hong Kong was a British colony and had been for about 80 years, so it had this strange British/Chinese mix that was unlike anywhere else. Of course, I didn't think *anything* about my childhood or my neighbourhood was strange at the time, but I realised once I started to travel the world in my 20s that my school friends and I had lived through an extraordinary historic moment in Chinese culture that was to define my beliefs for the rest of my live.

Let me explain. Chinese traditional beliefs are deeply rooted in spirituality, astrology, and holistic medicine. Spirituality plays a central role in Chinese culture, with practices such as ancestor worship, Taoism, and Confucianism shaping societal norms and values. Astrology, including practices like Feng Shui and the Chinese zodiac, influences various aspects of daily life, from determining auspicious dates for events to guiding personal decisions. Alternative medicine, such as Traditional Chinese Medicine, focuses on restoring harmony and balance within the body through practices like acupuncture, herbal remedies, and Qi Gong. The concept of Chi, or vital energy, permeates Chinese thought, influencing everything from martial arts to emotional and mental wellbeing.

In contrast, British culture is characterised by its empirical approach to science, rigid law and order, and hierarchical social structure. Empirical science, with its emphasis on evidence-based reasoning and experimentation, forms the basis of modern British thought. The British legal system is known for its strict adherence to laws and regulations, ensuring social order and stability.

British society has historically been hierarchical, with a rigid class system based on birthright, wealth, and privilege and a strong emphasis on social class and status. This was directly opposed to the ideological foundations of Chinese communist culture which advocated for the abolition of private property, class struggle, and the establishment of a classless society, aiming to eliminate social hierarchies by promoting equality among individuals.

When Hong Kong became a British colony, it brought together these two distinct belief systems in a unique blend. The fusion of Chinese tradition and British culture created a vibrant and dynamic society where opposites attracted and complemented each other. In Hong Kong, traditional Chinese beliefs found a way to coexist alongside British legal frameworks, resulting in a complex cultural landscape where Eastern and Western influences converged.

Despite their inherent differences, the spiritual and holistic aspects of Chinese tradition provided a counterbalance to the empirical and hierarchical aspects of British culture. This blending of opposites created a harmonious equilibrium that defined the cultural identity of Hong Kong—and my childhood values and beliefs. The city became a melting pot of diverse beliefs and practices, where Eastern philosophies and Western principles intertwined to create a unique and vibrant cultural landscape.

This dynamic interplay between East and West in Hong Kong exemplifies the Yin and Yang principle, where opposites attract and balance each other, creating a harmonious and culturally rich society.

One of the first things the British did when they leased Hong Kong for 99 years in 1898 was to remodel existing buildings at Tai Kwun in Central into a modern prison. As a small child in the 1970s, I remember riding the bus along Hollywood Road past this huge stone jail and seeing prisoners in the yard, exercising and waving back at us school children. When the lease was up and the

British left in 1997, the decommissioned prison eventually became Tai Kwun Arts Centre.

Whilst not strictly as simple as the British opting for penal control and the Chinese opting for artistic freedom, I do love this convenient symbolism of the difference in beliefs and cultures. It's yet another example of Yin and Yang that continues to influence my life.

Yin and Yang is described as the complementary and interconnected forces or principles representing opposing yet interdependent aspects of the universe, such as light and dark, hot and cold, active and passive, and female and male, symbolising harmony and balance.

While Yin and Yang are not exclusively defined as "female" and "male," and either sex can be considered Yin or Yang within a given context, in terms of their most general relation to one another, Yin references the female and Yang the male. This mirrors my beliefs about my own gender. Whilst I identify as neither male nor female, at the same time I identify with the *spirit* of both. Since I am a believer and lifelong practitioner of Chi—the life-force that *balances* Yin and Yang—I choose to be mindful of both sides in order to find true balance and harmony. Perhaps this identifies me as Chi-Gender?

I believe the particular events of my formative years—and a life dedicated to the understanding and teachings of Chi—have given me a unique perspective on life. In the following pages, I hope to teach you about the powerful force of Chi and give you the tools to bring out your true inner self. Along the way, I will guide you through your journey and set you up for a lifetime of inner strength, self-control and deep happiness.

I am honoured to share my knowledge with you.

Wishing you strength and light,

Rita Pei Lee

CHAPTER 1

INTRODUCTION TO CHI

Chi, pronounced "chee" in English, is everywhere. It's the life force that powers every living being, including you. Call it your spirit, a divine energy, or those feelings that make you, you, some of us have strong Chi that makes us confident, unafraid of challenges and super ambitious—life's winners in love, health, happiness and success. For those of you who aren't like that, I have good news. You can develop and strengthen your Chi (we call it "balancing") to achieve whatever you want in life.

It won't happen overnight and it takes some effort on your part, but once you see the changes in yourself and you start to include Chi practices as part of your daily routine, there will be no stopping you. And it's not just the final destination that makes Chi so rewarding, it's also the journey along the way that can be empowering. Chi will build your confidence, reduce your anxiety, help you focus and overcome any self-doubts you have.

On our journey, you'll learn how to find and balance your Chi through specific practices, exercises, routines and products, but first you must be positive and believe in this incredible life journey you're about to take.

Think of me as your travel buddy, showing you the best sights, the hidden places that only the locals know about (and the sketchy parts of town to avoid). So leave any negativity behind and let's begin our journey.

What is Chi? A Conceptual Overview

In order to fully grasp the essence of Chi, it's imperative to look into its conceptual framework and understand its significance in various cultural and philosophical contexts. Chi is an ancient Chinese concept that represents the fundamental life force or energy that permeates all living beings and the universe itself. This vital energy is believed to flow through pathways known as meridians, influencing physical, mental, and spiritual wellbeing.

The concept of Chi is deeply rooted in traditional Chinese philosophy and medicine, dating back thousands of years. It forms the cornerstone of many ancient practices such as Tai Chi, Qi Gong, Acupuncture, and Traditional Chinese Medicine (TCM). While the term Chi itself may vary across different Asian cultures, the underlying principle of vital energy remains consistent.

At its core, Chi represents the dynamic balance and interplay between complementary forces, known as Yin and Yang, within the body and the cosmos. This balance is essential for optimal health and harmony, with disruptions in Chi flow believed to lead to illness, disease, and imbalance.

Throughout history, Chi has been described and conceptualised in various ways, reflecting its multifaceted nature and diverse interpretations. In traditional Chinese philosophy, Chi is often associated with vitality, resilience, and the interconnectedness of all things. It encompasses both tangible and intangible aspects of existence, including physical energy, emotions, thoughts, and consciousness.

In the context of Traditional Chinese Medicine, Chi serves as a foundational concept guiding diagnosis, treatment, and preventive care. Practitioners of TCM seek to harmonise and balance the flow of Chi within the body through various modalities, including Aromatherapy, Acupuncture, Herbal Medicine, Dietary Therapy, and Therapeutic Exercise.

Moreover, Chi is deeply intertwined with spiritual and metaphysical beliefs in many Eastern traditions, where it is seen as a source of spiritual enlightenment, inner wisdom, and transcendence. Practices such as meditation, mindfulness, and breathwork are employed to cultivate and refine one's Chi, leading to enhanced awareness, clarity, and spiritual growth.

While the concept of Chi may seem abstract or esoteric to some, its practical implications are far-reaching and profound. By understanding and harnessing the power of Chi, we all can cultivate greater vitality, resilience, and overall wellbeing. This holistic approach emphasises the interconnectedness of mind, body, and spirit, recognising the importance of balance and harmony in all aspects of life.

Chi has fascinated scholars, philosophers, and practitioners for centuries. At its core, Chi is often described as the vital life force that animates all living beings and permeates the universe. While its origins date back to ancient China, similar concepts of life force energy exist in various cultures and traditions worldwide, albeit with different names and interpretations.

The term Chi itself is derived from the Chinese word 氣, which is pronounced as "Qi" in Mandarin and "Ki" in Japanese. It is considered the foundation of Traditional Chinese Medicine, martial arts, meditation practices, and Feng Shui.

One of the fundamental principles of Chi is its dynamic nature, constantly flowing and changing in response to internal and external factors. In traditional Chinese philosophy, Yin and Yang represent the complementary forces that govern the universe, with Chi serving as the medium through which these forces interact and maintain balance. It is this balance that is crucial for overall health and wellbeing.

In the context of health, Chi is intricately linked to blood and bodily fluids, which are vital for maintaining physiological functions and supporting the body's natural healing processes. Traditional Chinese Medicine views illness as a manifestation of imbalances or disruptions in the flow of Chi, and treatments often aim to restore harmony and balance to the body's energy system.

Beyond its physiological implications, Chi also encompasses mental, emotional, and spiritual aspects of human experience. In traditional Chinese thought, emotions are closely connected to specific organs and meridians, with imbalances in emotional energy believed to affect corresponding physical organs and vice versa. Practices such as meditation, breathwork, and Tai Chi are designed to cultivate awareness of Chi and promote its free flow throughout the body, mind, and spirit.

The principles of Chi have been increasingly recognised and integrated into contemporary wellness practices worldwide. From Acupuncture and Acupressure to Tai Chi and Qi Gong, a growing body of scientific research supports the effectiveness of Chi-based therapies in promoting health, reducing stress, and enhancing overall wellbeing.

In recent years, the concept of Chi has also gained popularity in Western cultures, where it is often referred to as "vital energy," "life force," or "bioenergy." This growing interest has led to the integration of Chi-based practices into various fields, including healthcare, psychology, sports performance, and personal development.

In summary, Chi represents a holistic understanding of life force energy that encompasses the interconnectedness of body, mind, and spirit. By cultivating awareness of Chi and nurturing its flow through mindful practices, you can enhance your vitality, resilience, and overall quality of life.

The Historical Roots of Chi

We can trace Chi back to ancient China, where it emerged as a central concept in various philosophical, medical, and spiritual traditions. Dating back thousands of years, the concept of Chi has undergone evolution and refinement, shaping the cultural and intellectual landscape of Chinese civilisation.

In ancient Chinese philosophy, the concept of Chi was first articulated in texts such as the *I Ching* or *Book of Changes* and the *Tao Te Ching* by Laozi. These foundational texts laid the groundwork for understanding Chi as the fundamental life force that permeates all aspects of existence. According to the *Tao Te Ching*, Chi is the source of all creation and the underlying principle of harmony and balance in the universe. As Chinese civilisation flourished, the concept of Chi continued to evolve and expand, finding expression in various philosophical schools such as Confucianism, Taoism, and Neo-Confucianism. Each of these traditions offered unique perspectives on Chi, emphasising its role in human nature, society, and the cosmos.

In Taoism, Chi is central to the concept of Tao, or the Way, which represents the natural order of the universe. According to Taoist teachings, cultivating Chi through practices such as meditation, breathwork, and Tai Chi allows individuals to align themselves with the flow of Tao and attain a state of harmony and balance.

In Confucianism, Chi is associated with the concept of "De", which encompasses virtues such as benevolence, righteousness, and propriety. Confucian teachings emphasise the cultivation of Chi through ethical conduct and moral character, believing that a harmonious society arises from individuals embodying virtuous qualities.

The historical development of Chi in Chinese culture also intersected with various other cultural practices and belief systems. For example, martial arts such as Tai Chi and Qi Gong incorporate principles of Chi cultivation, emphasising the integration of mind, body, and spirit in combat and self-defence.

Moreover, Chi found expression in traditional Chinese arts such as calligraphy, painting, and music, where practitioners sought to embody the dynamic flow of Chi through their creative expression. The concept of Chi also influenced architectural design, Feng Shui principles, and agricultural practices, reflecting its pervasive influence on all aspects of Chinese life.

In summary, the historical roots of Chi are deeply intertwined with the cultural, philosophical, and spiritual heritage of ancient China. From its earliest articulations in philosophical texts to its integration into various aspects of Chinese life, Chi has remained a fundamental concept that continues to shape our understanding of health, harmony, and the human experience.

Modern Interpretations of Chi

In recent times, the concept of Chi has transcended its traditional roots in Chinese philosophy and medicine, finding resonance in various contemporary disciplines and cultures worldwide. Modern interpretations of Chi reflect a nuanced understanding of this vital life force energy, integrating ancient wisdom with contemporary insights.

Here, we explore how Chi is perceived and applied in different contexts, shedding light on its evolving significance in the modern world.

Holistic Health and Wellness

In the realm of holistic health and wellness, Chi plays a central role as a guiding principle for achieving balance and vitality. Many alternative healing modalities, such as Acupuncture, Reiki, and Qi Gong, are based on the premise of harmonising Chi flow within the body to promote physical, emotional, and spiritual wellbeing. These practices emphasise the interconnectedness of mind, body, and spirit, viewing health as a dynamic equilibrium of Chi energy.

Moreover, contemporary wellness trends increasingly incorporate Chi-based approaches to address various health concerns and enhance overall vitality. From Chi-infused products like herbal supplements and Aromatherapy oils to Chi-centred therapies like Tai Chi and mindfulness meditation, individuals are exploring diverse avenues to optimise their Chi flow and cultivate a state of holistic wellness.

Mind-Body Practices

In the realm of mind-body practices, Chi serves as a guiding principle for cultivating awareness, presence, and vitality. Practices such as yoga, Tai Chi, and Qi Gong emphasise the cultivation of Chi flow through mindful movement, breathwork, and meditation. By attuning to the subtle rhythms of Chi energy within the body, practitioners aim to harmonise their internal landscape, promoting physical health, mental clarity, and emotional balance.

Moreover, modern interpretations of Chi extend beyond traditional Eastern disciplines to encompass a wide range of mind-body modalities rooted in mindfulness, somatic awareness, and energy healing. Practices like mindfulness-based stress reduction (MBSR), breathwork therapy, and bioenergetic healing integrate Chi principles into Western therapeutic frameworks, offering innovative approaches to holistic wellbeing.

Creative Expression and Embodied Arts

Within the realms of creative expression and embodied arts, Chi serves as a source of inspiration and vitality, fuelling artistic creativity and embodied expression. Many artists, dancers, musicians, and performers draw upon Chi energy as a source of creative inspiration, tapping into its flow to channel their artistic expression.

Moreover, Chi-based practices like dance therapy, somatic movement, and expressive arts therapy provide avenues for individuals to explore and embody their inner Chi energy through creative expression. By engaging in spontaneous movement, expressive gestures, and embodied storytelling, participants can access deeper layers of their psyche and tap into the transformative power of Chi energy for healing and self-discovery.

Environmental Sustainability and Conscious Living

In the realm of environmental sustainability and conscious living, Chi serves as a guiding principle for harmonising human activities with the natural world, fostering ecological balance and planetary wellbeing. Many environmentalists, ecologists, and sustainability advocates recognise the interconnectedness of all life forms and the vital importance of Chi energy in sustaining ecosystems and biodiversity.

Moreover, Chi-based practices like permaculture, forest bathing, and mindful eco-living offer practical tools for cultivating a deeper connection with nature and promoting sustainable living practices. By aligning human activities with the natural rhythms of Chi energy, individuals can contribute to the regeneration of the Earth and the preservation of its vital ecosystems for future generations.

Integrative Medicine and Healing Arts

Within integrative medicine and healing arts, Chi serves as a foundational principle for addressing the root causes of illness and promoting holistic healing. Integrative healthcare approaches, which combine conventional medicine with complementary and alternative therapies, often incorporate Chi-based modalities to support patients' overall wellbeing and enhance treatment outcomes.

Practitioners of integrative medicine recognise the importance of Chi energy in maintaining health and vitality, viewing illness as a manifestation of imbalances within the body's energy systems. By integrating Chi-based therapies such as acupuncture, herbal medicine, and energy healing into their treatment protocols, healthcare providers aim to restore the body's natural flow of Chi and support the innate healing processes.

Moreover, Chi-based approaches are increasingly being integrated into mainstream healthcare settings, with hospitals, clinics, and wellness centres offering services such as acupuncture, Tai Chi, and mindfulness meditation as adjunct therapies for managing various health conditions. This shift toward integrative healthcare reflects a growing recognition of the interconnectedness of mind, body, and spirit in promoting optimal health and wellbeing.

Quantum Physics and Energy Medicine

Chi finds resonance with cutting-edge scientific theories and research on the nature of energy and consciousness. Quantum physicists and energy healers alike explore the profound implications of quantum mechanics for understanding the underlying dynamics of Chi energy and its influence on human health and consciousness.

From the perspective of quantum physics, Chi can be conceptualised as a subtle energy field that permeates all living organisms and interacts with the quantum field of the universe. This view aligns with the ancient wisdom of Chinese philosophy, which describes Chi as the vital life force that animates all forms of life and connects them to the cosmic energy matrix.

Moreover, energy medicine modalities such as biofield therapies, frequency-based healing, and subtle energy interventions draw upon the principles of Chi energy to facilitate healing at the quantum level. By harnessing the inherent intelligence of the body's energy systems, practitioners of energy medicine aim to catalyse profound shifts in health and consciousness, promoting holistic healing and transformation.

Cultural and Cross-Cultural Perspectives

Chi serves as a unifying concept that transcends cultural boundaries and bridges diverse traditions and belief systems. While rooted in ancient Chinese philosophy and culture, the concept of Chi has permeated various cultures and civilisations throughout history, manifesting in different forms and expressions.

Across cultures, Chi is known by various names and conceptualised in diverse ways, reflecting the unique cultural lenses through which it is understood and experienced. From the Indian concept of Prana to the Japanese notion of Ki, from the Polynesian concept of Mana to the Native American concept of Spirit Energy, Chi finds expression in a rich tapestry of cultural beliefs and practices worldwide.

Moreover, the globalisation of knowledge and the exchange of ideas have facilitated the cross-pollination of Chi-based practices and perspectives across different cultural contexts. Today, individuals from diverse cultural backgrounds have access to a wealth of Chi-based wisdom and practices, enriching their lives and expanding their understanding of the universal principles of vitality, balance, and harmony.

In summary, modern interpretations of Chi encompass a broad spectrum of disciplines and perspectives, reflecting its multi-faceted nature and universal relevance in the contemporary world. Whether explored through the lens of holistic health, quantum physics, cultural studies, or integrative medicine, Chi offers a profound framework for understanding and cultivating vitality, balance, and harmony in all aspects of life.

The Importance of Chi in Personal Development

Chi, as a fundamental concept in traditional Chinese philosophy and medicine, holds profound significance in the realm of personal development. In this section, we will explore the role of Chi in fostering growth, resilience, and self-actualisation (manifesting), highlighting its importance as a guiding principle for individuals seeking to enhance their wellbeing and fulfilment.

Cultivating Vitality and Energy

One of the primary benefits of cultivating Chi in personal development is the enhancement of vitality and energy. As I've previously mentioned, Chi is often referred to as the life force energy that animates all living beings, serving as the source of vitality, resilience, and overall wellbeing. By cultivating Chi through various practices such as Qi Gong, Tai Chi, and breathwork, we can tap into this reservoir of energy to replenish our physical, mental, and emotional vitality.

Through regular Chi cultivation practices, we can experience increased energy levels, improved stamina, and a greater sense of vitality in our daily lives. This heightened energy state not only enhances physical health and performance but also contributes to mental clarity, emotional balance, and overall resilience in the face of life's challenges.

Balancing Mind, Body, and Spirit

Another key aspect of Chi in personal development is its role in balancing the mind, body, and spirit. In Traditional Chinese Medicine and philosophy, health is viewed as a state of dynamic balance and harmony between the various aspects of the individual, including the physical body, emotions, thoughts, and spirit.

Chi serves as the medium through which this balance and harmony are maintained, facilitating the free flow of energy throughout the body-mind-spirit system. Through practices such as acupuncture, Acupressure, and energy healing, we can address imbalances in our energy system and restore harmony within ourselves.

By cultivating Chi and promoting energetic balance, we can experience greater alignment between our thoughts, emotions, and actions, leading to a deeper sense of inner peace, clarity, and purpose in life. This holistic approach to personal development emphasises the interconnectedness of mind, body, and spirit and empowers us to cultivate wellbeing on all levels of our being.

Enhancing Resilience and Adaptability

Chi cultivation practices also play a crucial role in enhancing resilience and adaptability in personal development. In today's fast-paced and often stressful world, we are constantly faced with challenges, setbacks, and uncertainties that can undermine our wellbeing and sense of self-efficacy.

By cultivating Chi through practices such as mindfulness meditation, breathwork, and energy healing, we can develop greater resilience and adaptability in the face of adversity. Chi serves as a source of inner strength and resilience, enabling us to navigate life's challenges with grace, equanimity, and resourcefulness.

Through regular Chi cultivation practices, we can develop greater emotional resilience, cognitive flexibility, and adaptive coping strategies, allowing us to thrive in the face of adversity and emerge stronger and more resilient from life's trials and tribulations.

Fostering Self-Actualisation, Manifestation and Fulfilment

Finally, Chi cultivation plays a vital role in fostering self-actualisation, manifestation and fulfilment in personal development. Self-actualisation, as defined by psychologist Abraham Maslow, refers to the realisation of one's full potential and the fulfilment of one's deepest aspirations and desires.

Chi serves as a catalyst for self-actualisation, empowering us to tap into our innate potential and manifest our unique gifts, talents, and passions in the world. By cultivating Chi through practices such as mindfulness meditation, energy healing, and creative expression, we can awaken to our true nature, unleash our creative potential, and live authentically from the depths of our being.

Through the cultivation of Chi, we can align with our life purpose, express our authentic selves, and experience a deep sense of meaning in our lives. Chi serves as a guiding principle for personal development, leading individuals on a journey of self-discovery, growth, and transformation toward a life of greater vitality, balance, and fulfilment.

Cultivating Emotional Intelligence and Wellbeing

In addition to physical vitality and mental clarity, cultivating Chi is also instrumental in fostering emotional intelligence and wellbeing. Emotional intelligence refers to the ability to recognise, understand, and manage one's own emotions, as well as to empathise with and navigate the emotions of others effectively.

Through mindfulness meditation, we learn to observe our thoughts and emotions with non-judgmental awareness, allowing us to respond to challenging situations with greater clarity and equanimity. Energy healing practices such as Reiki and Qi Gong facilitate the release of emotional blockages and traumas stored in the body, promoting emotional healing and balance.

Enhancing Spiritual Growth and Connection

Finally, Chi cultivation plays a crucial role in enhancing spiritual growth and connection in personal development. Spirituality refers to the innate human need for meaning, purpose, and connection to something greater than oneself, whether it be a higher power, universal consciousness, or the interconnected web of life.

Chi serves as a bridge between the physical and spiritual dimensions of human experience, facilitating a deeper connection to the inherent sacredness of life and the interconnectedness of all beings. Through practices such as meditation, energy healing, and mindfulness, we can cultivate Chi and deepen our spiritual connection.

By cultivating Chi, we can awaken to our innate spiritual nature, deepen our connection to the divine, and experience a profound sense of inner peace, purpose, and fulfilment. Chi serves as a guiding principle for spiritual growth and connection, leading us on a journey of self-discovery, awakening, and transcendence.

In conclusion, the cultivation of Chi plays a vital role in personal development, fostering vitality, balance, resilience, and fulfilment on all levels of being. By cultivating Chi through various practices such as mindfulness meditation, energy healing, and breathwork, we can tap into our inner resources, awaken our full potential, and live authentically from the depths of our being. Chi serves as a guiding principle for personal growth and transformation, empowering us to thrive in body, mind, and spirit, and to lead lives of greater vitality, balance, and meaning.

CHAPTER 2

FOUNDATIONS OF CHI

In exploring the concept of Chi, we inevitably encounter its deep philosophical underpinnings, rooted in ancient Chinese philosophy and culture. The philosophical foundation of Chi provides invaluable insights into its essence, significance, and practical applications in daily life.

Chi holds a central place in Chinese philosophy, particularly in Daoism and Confucianism. Daoism, one of the major philosophical traditions in China, emphasises the harmony between humanity and nature, seeking to align with the natural flow of life. Central to Daoist philosophy is the notion of Chi, which permeates all aspects of existence, from the cosmos to the human body. According to Daoist teachings, cultivating and harmonising one's Chi leads to good health, longevity, and spiritual enlightenment.

Confucianism, another influential school of thought in China, also acknowledges the importance of Chi, albeit in a slightly different context. Confucian philosophy emphasises moral cultivation, social harmony, and virtuous conduct.

Chi, within the Confucian framework, is associated with ethical vitality and inner strength, essential for leading a meaningful and purposeful life.

In this chapter, I'll share the solid foundations of Chi that have shaped my lifelong belief, and the undeniable effects that Chi can have on modern life.

The Philosophical Underpinnings of Chi

The philosophical underpinnings of Chi extend beyond Daoism and Confucianism to include other Chinese philosophical traditions, such as Buddhism and Legalism. While interpretations may vary, the underlying concept of Chi remains a common thread, symbolising the interconnectedness of all phenomena and the dynamic interplay of complementary forces.

Ancient Chinese philosophers, including Laozi, Zhuangzi, and Confucius, offered profound insights into the nature of Chi and its role in shaping human experience. Their writings and teachings continue to inspire contemporary interpretations of Chi, fostering a deeper understanding of life's mysteries and possibilities.

As we dig into the philosophical underpinnings of Chi, we encounter fundamental questions about the nature of existence, the relationship between mind and body, and the pursuit of inner harmony. These philosophical inquiries serve as a springboard for exploring the multifaceted dimensions of Chi and its profound implications for personal growth and holistic wellbeing.

As a philosophical concept, Chi transcends cultural boundaries and resonates with universal themes of vitality, balance, and interconnectedness. By embracing the philosophical underpinnings of Chi, we embark on a transformative journey of self-discovery, aligning with the natural rhythms of life and tapping into the boundless potential of the human spirit.

As we navigate the complexities of modern life, the timeless wisdom of ancient Chinese philosophy offers invaluable guidance and inspiration. By reflecting on the philosophical underpinnings of Chi, we gain a deeper appreciation for the intricate tapestry of existence and the enduring quest for harmony and enlightenment.

Throughout history, various philosophical traditions have explored the concept of Chi, offering unique perspectives on its nature and significance. In this section, we examine how different philosophical frameworks have shaped our understanding of our vital life force.

Ancient Chinese Philosophy

The roots of Chi can be traced back to ancient Chinese philosophy, particularly within the Daoist and Confucian traditions. In Daoism, Chi is viewed as the fundamental essence that permeates all of existence, representing the dynamic flow of energy that sustains life. Daoist texts such as the *Dao De Jing* emphasise the importance of aligning with the natural flow of Chi to achieve harmony and balance. Similarly, in Confucianism, Chi is regarded as the vital force that animates human beings and the universe, guiding ethical conduct and social harmony. The Confucian concept of "Li" refers to the pattern or order inherent in the natural world, which is sustained by the flow of Chi.

Greek Philosophy

While the concept of Chi is unique to Chinese philosophy, parallels can be drawn to certain aspects of Greek philosophy, particularly the notion of Pneuma in Stoicism and Aristotelian metaphysics. Pneuma, meaning "breath" or "vital spirit," shares similarities with Chi in its role as the animating force that permeates all of existence. Stoic philosophers such as Zeno and Seneca viewed Pneuma as the divine principle that governs the universe and guides human conduct. Similarly, Aristotle's concept of "Entelechy," which refers to the inherent purpose or potentiality within living beings, bears resemblance to the notion of Chi as the vital energy that drives growth and development.

Indian Philosophy

In Indian philosophical traditions such as Hinduism and Buddhism, similar concepts to Chi are found, albeit under different names. In Hindu philosophy, the concept of "Prana" refers to the vital life force that sustains all living beings and permeates the universe. Prana is believed to flow through subtle energy channels known as Nadis, influencing physical, mental, and spiritual wellbeing. Similarly, in Buddhism, the concept of Prana or Vayu denotes the vital energy that animates sentient beings and is essential for spiritual practice and enlightenment.

Western Philosophy

While Western philosophy does not have an exact equivalent to the concept of Chi, there are philosophical ideas that resonate with its principles. For example, the concept of "Vitalism", which posits the existence of a vital life force or energy that distinguishes living organisms from inanimate matter, shares similarities with Chi. Philosophers such as Henri Bergson and Friedrich Schelling explored vitalist ideas in their works, emphasising the dynamic and creative nature of life.

In summary, the philosophical underpinnings of Chi encompass a diverse range of traditions and perspectives, each offering valuable insights into the nature of this vital life force. From ancient Chinese philosophy to Greek, Indian, and Western philosophical traditions, the concept of Chi reflects humanity's enduring quest to understand the fundamental principles underlying existence.

Traditional Chinese Medicine and Chi

Traditional Chinese Medicine stands as a testament to the richness of ancient healing practices that have flourished in China for thousands of years. Embedded within the core of Traditional Chinese Medicine lies the profound concept of Chi as an intricate and multifaceted principle that serves as the cornerstone of health and vitality in Chinese philosophy and culture. In this section, we delve into the depths of Traditional Chinese Medicine to unravel the intricate relationship between Chi and the holistic approach to wellbeing.

Understanding Chi in Traditional Chinese Medicine

At the heart of Traditional Chinese Medicine lies the fundamental belief in the existence of Chi as the animating essence that sustains all living beings and orchestrates the intricate dance of physiological processes within the body. In the realm of Traditional Chinese Medicine, the smooth and harmonious flow of Chi is regarded as the quintessential element for maintaining health and vitality, while disruptions or imbalances in Chi flow are seen as the root cause of illness and disease.

According to Traditional Chinese Medicine theory, Chi circulates through a complex network of channels known as meridians, traversing the body in a continuous and interconnected web. These meridians serve as the conduits through which Chi flows, influencing the functions of organs and tissues, regulating bodily processes, and supporting the body's natural healing mechanisms. Each meridian is associated with specific organs and bodily functions, and the smooth flow of Chi through these channels is crucial for maintaining optimal health and wellbeing.

Balancing Chi

Within Traditional Chinese Medicine, the ultimate goal of healing is to restore balance and harmony to the body by harmonising the flow of Chi. Traditional Chinese Medicine practitioners employ a diverse array of therapeutic modalities aimed at correcting imbalances in Chi flow, addressing disharmonies in the body, and promoting the body's innate capacity for self-healing.

Acupuncture, perhaps the most renowned therapeutic modality within Traditional Chinese Medicine, is based on the principle of regulating Chi flow by inserting fine needles into specific points along the body's meridian pathways. By stimulating these acupuncture points, practitioners aim to remove blockages, tonify deficient Chi, disperse excess Chi, and restore balance to the body's energy systems. Acupuncture has been shown to be effective in addressing a wide range of health conditions, from pain management and stress reduction to supporting emotional wellbeing and enhancing overall vitality.

Herbal medicine, another integral component of Traditional Chinese Medicine, harnesses the healing power of medicinal plants, minerals, and animal products to regulate Chi flow, nourish vital organs, and address specific health concerns. Herbal formulas are meticulously crafted to target individual patterns of Chi imbalance, constitution, and presenting symptoms, offering a personalised approach to healing that addresses the root causes of illness and restores balance to the body.

Dietary therapy, an often-overlooked aspect of Traditional Chinese Medicine, plays a pivotal role in supporting Chi flow and promoting overall wellbeing. According to Traditional Chinese Medicine principles, certain foods possess inherent energetic properties that can influence the flow of Chi within the body. By incorporating Chi-balancing foods into our diet and avoiding foods that disrupt Chi flow, we can support our body's natural healing mechanisms and cultivate vibrant health from within.

Promoting Chi Flow

In addition to Acupuncture, herbal medicine, and dietary therapy, Traditional Chinese Medicine encompasses a diverse array of mind-body practices aimed at promoting the smooth flow of Chi and enhancing overall wellbeing. Qi Gong (气功), a system of gentle movements, breathing exercises, and meditation, is one such practice that holds profound implications for cultivating Chi, reducing stress, and supporting emotional balance.

Qi Gong, which translates to "cultivating energy" or "working with the breath", encompasses a wide range of practices that are designed to harmonise Chi flow, cultivate internal energy, and promote health and longevity. Through gentle movements, mindful breathing, and meditative awareness, practitioners of Qi Gong can tap into the body's innate reservoir of Chi, promoting vitality, resilience, and wellbeing.

Tai Chi (太极拳), another renowned practice rooted in Traditional Chinese Medicine, embodies the principles of balance, harmony and flow. Often described as "meditation in motion," Tai Chi combines slow, graceful movements with deep breathing and mindfulness to promote Chi flow, improve balance, and strengthen the body's internal energy. Regular practice of Tai Chi has been shown to enhance physical health, reduce stress, and foster a profound sense of wellbeing.

Chi and Emotional Health

In the realm of Traditional Chinese Medicine, Chi is not merely viewed as the vital energy that sustains physical health but also as the subtle force that underlies emotional wellbeing. According to Traditional Chinese Medicine theory, imbalances in Chi flow can manifest as emotional disturbances such as anxiety, depression or irritability, highlighting the intricate interplay between Chi and emotional health.

Traditional Chinese Medicine treatments aimed at harmonising Chi flow can have profound effects on emotional wellbeing, helping to alleviate stress, calm the mind, and restore emotional balance. Acupuncture, herbal medicine, Aromatherapy, Qi Gong, and Tai Chi are all esteemed for their ability to support mental and emotional wellbeing by promoting the free flow of Chi throughout the body, fostering a deep sense of inner peace, and cultivating emotional resilience.

In summary, Traditional Chinese Medicine offers a holistic approach to health and healing that revolves around the concept of Chi. By regulating Chi flow through acupuncture, herbal medicine, Aromatherapy, dietary therapy, and mind-body practices such as Qi Gong and Tai Chi, Traditional Chinese Medicine aims to support the body's innate healing abilities, restore balance and harmony to the body, and promote overall wellbeing on physical, emotional, and spiritual levels.

Scientific Perspectives on Chi

In the realm of modern science, the concept of Chi has often been met with skepticism due to its abstract and metaphysical nature. However, in recent years, there has been a growing interest in exploring the scientific underpinnings of Chi and its potential implications for health and wellbeing. In this section, we dive into the scientific perspectives on Chi, examining research findings and exploring emerging areas of inquiry that shed light on the physiological and psychological mechanisms underlying this ancient concept.

The Science of Energy Medicine

One of the key areas of scientific inquiry related to Chi revolves around the field of energy medicine, which explores the role of subtle energy fields in health and healing. Energy medicine encompasses a diverse array of modalities, including biofield therapies, electromagnetic therapies, and mind-body practices, all of which are grounded in the premise that subtle energy fields influence physiological processes and play a role in maintaining health.

Research in energy medicine has provided compelling evidence supporting the existence of bioenergetic fields within and around the human body. Techniques such as biofield imaging, Kirlian photography, and electrodermal screening have demonstrated the presence of electromagnetic fields and subtle energy patterns associated with acupuncture points, meridians, and other energy centres in the body. These findings lend credence to the concept of Chi as a bioenergetic phenomenon that can be objectively measured and studied using scientific methods.

Neurophysiological Correlates of Chi

Another area of scientific inquiry related to Chi revolves around exploring the neurophysiological correlates of Chi and its effects on the brain and nervous system. Research in neuroscience has revealed fascinating insights into the effects of mind-body practices such as meditation, Qi Gong, and Tai Chi on brain function, demonstrating their ability to modulate neural activity, promote neuroplasticity, and enhance cognitive function.

Studies using advanced neuroimaging techniques such as Functional magnetic resonance imaging (fMRI) and Electroencephalography (EEG) have shown that practices that cultivate Chi, such as meditation and Qi Gong, can induce profound changes in brain structure and function. These practices have been associated with increased activity in brain regions involved in attention, emotional regulation, and self-awareness, as well as alterations in brainwave patterns indicative of relaxed states and heightened states of consciousness.

Physiological Effects of Chi Practices

Beyond the realm of neuroscience, research has also explored the physiological effects of Chi practices on the body, shedding light on the mechanisms underlying their therapeutic benefits. Studies examining the effects of Acupuncture, Qi Gong, and Tai Chi have revealed a wide range of physiological changes associated with these practices, including alterations in hormone levels, immune function, and cardiovascular health.

Acupuncture, for example, has been shown to modulate the release of endogenous opioids and neurotransmitters, such as serotonin and dopamine, which play a key role in pain modulation and mood regulation. Qi Gong and Tai Chi, on the other hand, have been associated with improvements in cardiovascular function, immune function, and stress resilience, as well as reductions in inflammation and oxidative stress.

The Role of the Mind-Body Connection

Central to the scientific understanding of Chi is the recognition of the intricate interplay between the mind and body in shaping health and wellbeing. Research in psychoneuroimmunology, the study of the interactions between the mind, nervous system, and immune system, has provided compelling evidence supporting the role of mind-body practices in modulating immune function, reducing stress, and promoting overall health.

Practices that cultivate Chi have been shown to exert profound effects on the mind-body connection, influencing psychological factors such as stress, anxiety, and mood, as well as physiological parameters such as heart rate, blood pressure, and immune function. By fostering a deep sense of relaxation, inner peace, and emotional resilience, these practices support the body's innate healing mechanisms and promote holistic wellbeing.

In summary, scientific perspectives on Chi offer valuable insights into the physiological and psychological mechanisms underlying this ancient concept. Research in energy medicine, neuroscience, and mind-body medicine has provided compelling evidence supporting the existence of bioenergetic fields, the neurophysiological correlates of Chi practices, and the role of the mind-body connection in shaping health and wellbeing. By bridging the gap between ancient wisdom and modern science, these perspectives contribute to our understanding of Chi as a holistic principle that encompasses the interconnection of mind, body, and spirit.

Cultural Significance of Chi

As the embodiment of life force, Chi holds profound cultural significance across various societies, particularly in East Asian cultures like China, Japan, and Korea. Throughout history, Chi has been an integral part of philosophical, spiritual, and medical practices, shaping the way people perceive and interact with the world around them.

In traditional Chinese culture, Chi is deeply intertwined with the concept of Yin and Yang, representing opposing yet complementary forces that govern the universe. This duality is evident in various aspects of Chinese culture, including philosophy, medicine, martial arts, and Feng Shui. Yin and Yang are believed to manifest in all aspects of life, influencing everything from the seasons and natural elements to human emotions and behaviour.

The concept of Chi also plays a central role in Traditional Chinese Medicine, where it is considered the vital energy that flows through the body's meridian channels, nourishing and sustaining life. According to Traditional Chinese Medicine principles, imbalances or blockages in the flow of Chi can lead to physical, emotional, or spiritual disharmony, resulting in illness or disease.

In Japanese culture, Chi is known as Ki or Qi, and it is similarly regarded as the life force that animates all living things. In traditional Japanese martial arts like Aikido and Karate, practitioners harness their Ki to achieve harmony, balance, and strength in their movements. Ki is also central to the practice of Reiki, a form of energy healing that aims to channel universal life force energy to promote healing and relaxation.

Similarly, in Korean culture, Chi is referred to as Gi or Ki, and it is considered the fundamental energy that sustains life and vitality. Korean traditional medicine, known as Hanbang, also recognises the importance of Chi in maintaining health and wellbeing. Herbal medicine, acupuncture, moxibustion, and other holistic therapies are used in Hanbang to regulate the flow of Chi and restore balance to the body.

Beyond East Asia, the concept of Chi has influenced various aspects of global culture, particularly in the realm of alternative and complementary medicine. Practices like Acupuncture, Tai Chi, Qi Gong, and Reiki have gained popularity worldwide, reflecting a growing interest in holistic approaches to health and wellness that honour the body's innate healing abilities and energetic balance.

In conclusion, in contemporary culture, the idea of Chi continues to inspire creativity, innovation, and exploration in diverse fields, including art, literature, philosophy, and personal development. The concept of Chi invites individuals to cultivate awareness, mindfulness, and connection with their inner selves and the world around them, fostering a deeper sense of vitality, harmony, and purpose in life.

CHAPTER 3

NAVIGATING MENTAL WELLBEING

In today's fast-paced and interconnected world, the mental wellbeing of young people has become a pressing concern. As we navigate through unprecedented challenges such as the global pandemic, social upheaval, and economic uncertainty, the toll on mental health is evident, particularly among young women. This chapter looks at the multifaceted aspects of mental wellbeing, focusing on emotional, social, and psychological dimensions.

Through an exploration of societal expectations, the impact of social media, peer relationships, and the importance of prioritising and seeking support for mental health, I aim to shed light on the growing mental health crisis among young women and empower them to navigate through life's challenges with resilience and self-care.

The Impact of Mental Health on Emotional Wellbeing

Emotional wellbeing is a critical component of overall mental health, yet young women are increasingly facing significant challenges in this area, exacerbating the growing mental health crisis. The emotional landscape of young women is fraught with complexities, influenced by a myriad of internal and external factors that shape their experiences and perceptions of self and others.

Social and cultural expectations place immense pressure on young women to embody certain emotional traits and behaviours, often at the expense of their authentic selves. The pressure to conform to societal norms of femininity, such as being nurturing, accommodating, and emotionally expressive, can create internal conflicts and feelings of inadequacy when young women deviate from these expectations. Additionally, societal stigma surrounding mental health issues may prevent young women from seeking help or expressing their emotional struggles openly, leading to feelings of isolation and alienation.

The pervasive influence of social media further complicates the emotional landscape for young women, exposing them to curated and often unrealistic portrayals of happiness, success, and fulfilment. Constant comparison with idealised images and lifestyles promoted on social media undeniably contributes to feelings of inadequacy, low self-esteem, and a diminished sense of self-worth among young women, perpetuating a cycle of emotional distress and dissatisfaction. From my own experiences, many cases I have overseen have a level of distress attributed to social media exposure.

Moreover, the challenges of navigating personal relationships, academic pressures, and career aspirations in an increasingly competitive and fast world can take a toll on the emotions of young women. Balancing multiple roles and responsibilities while striving to meet societal expectations and personal goals can lead to chronic stress, anxiety, and emotional exhaustion, further exacerbating mental health challenges.

The impact of emotional distress on young women is profound and far-reaching, affecting various aspects of their lives including academic performance, interpersonal relationships, and overall quality of life. Untreated emotional issues can manifest in physical symptoms such as headaches, digestive problems, and sleep disturbances, further exacerbating the cycle of distress and impairment in functioning.

Addressing the emotional wellbeing of young women requires a comprehensive approach that acknowledges and responds to the multifaceted nature of their experiences. This includes promoting self-awareness and emotional literacy to help young women recognise and express their feelings in healthy and constructive ways. Additionally, creating supportive and inclusive environments where young women feel validated and empowered to seek help and support for their emotional struggles is crucial in fostering resilience and promoting mental health.

Efforts to promote emotional wellbeing among young women must also address systemic barriers and inequities that contribute to disparities in access to mental health resources and support services. This includes advocating for policies and initiatives that prioritise mental health education, de-stigmatise seeking help for emotional issues, and increase accessibility to culturally competent and gender-sensitive mental health services for young women across diverse backgrounds and communities.

The Growing Mental Health Crisis Among Young Women

Mental health among young women is a pressing concern that demands further attention and action. Recent studies shed light on the alarming trends and factors contributing to this crisis, highlighting the urgent need for intervention and support.

Prevalence of Mental Health Disorders

According to the World Health Organisation (WHO), mental health disorders disproportionately affect young people, with half of all mental health conditions beginning by age 14 and three-quarters by age 24. Among these, mood disorders such as depression and anxiety are among the most prevalent, affecting young women at higher rates than their male counterparts.

A study published in the Journal of Abnormal Psychology found that rates of depression among adolescents and young adults have been steadily rising over the past decade, with young women experiencing a particularly pronounced increase in symptoms.

Social and Cultural Pressures

Young women today face unprecedented social and cultural pressures that can have detrimental effects on their mental health. The pressure to excel academically, succeed in their careers, maintain idealised body image standards, and navigate complex interpersonal relationships can create significant stress and anxiety. A survey conducted by the American Psychological Association (APA) found that young women report higher levels of stress compared to young men, citing concerns related to academic performance, appearance, and future prospects as primary sources of stress.

Impact of Social Media

The pervasive influence of social media has emerged as a significant factor contributing to the mental health crisis among young women. Research published in the Journal of Adolescent Health has found a strong correlation between social media use and symptoms of depression and anxiety among adolescents, with young women being particularly vulnerable to the negative effects of social media.

The constant exposure to carefully curated and often unrealistic portrayals of beauty, success, and happiness on social media platforms can fuel feelings of inadequacy, comparison, and low self-esteem among young women, exacerbating mental health issues.

Barriers to Accessing Mental Health Services

Despite the growing need for mental health support among young women, significant barriers exist that prevent them from accessing timely and adequate care. Stigma surrounding mental illness, particularly among young women, can discourage individuals from seeking help or disclosing their struggles to others. Moreover, structural barriers such as limited availability of mental health services, long wait times for appointments, and financial constraints can further impede access to care for young women, particularly those from marginalised communities.

Intersectional Identities and Unique Challenges

It is important to recognise that the mental health crisis among young women is not uniform and can vary based on intersecting identities such as race, ethnicity, sexual orientation, and socio-economic status. Young women from marginalised communities may face unique challenges and barriers to accessing mental health support, including systemic racism, discrimination, and lack of culturally competent care. Intersectional approaches to addressing mental health disparities are essential in ensuring that all young women receive the support and resources they need to thrive.

In summary, the growing mental health crisis among young people is a complex and multifaceted issue that requires a comprehensive and intersectional approach. By understanding the prevalence of mental health disorders, acknowledging social and cultural pressures, addressing the impact of social media, dismantling barriers to accessing mental health services, and recognising the intersectional identities and unique challenges faced by young women, we can work towards promoting mental health and wellbeing for all.

Societal Expectations and Their Impact on Mental Health

The burgeoning mental health crisis among young women is intricately intertwined with societal expectations that dictate norms of behaviour, appearance, and achievement. In today's society, young women are bombarded with unrealistic standards propagated by media, peer groups, and cultural narratives, exacerbating the pressure to conform and perform according to predetermined ideals.

Unrealistic Beauty Standards

Society often imposes narrow definitions of beauty, promoting unrealistic and unattainable body ideals that young women are expected to emulate. Mainstream media, fashion industries, and social media platforms perpetuate these standards through airbrushed images and curated lifestyles, leading to body dissatisfaction, low self-esteem, and disordered eating behaviours among young women.

According to a study by the National Eating Disorders Association (NEDA), 42% of girls in school grades 1-3 (five to eight year olds) want to be thinner, and 81% of 10-year-olds are afraid of being fat.

Let's just pause for a moment and digest that last sentence. It breaks my heart to write it but it's sadly a symptom of today's society. Ask your mom or your aunt if they were scared of being fat when they were 10 years old. I'm pretty certain what the answer will be.

Academic and Career Pressures

The relentless pursuit of academic excellence and career success adds another layer of stress and anxiety for young women. Despite making significant strides in education and workforce participation, young women continue to face gender disparities in opportunities for advancement and recognition. The pressure to excel academically and professionally while juggling multiple responsibilities can lead to burnout, imposter syndrome, and heightened levels of stress among young women. According to a survey by the American Psychological Association (APA), 61% of young adults reported stress about work, money, or the economy, and 39% reported stress related to academic performance.

Expectations of Emotional Labour

Young women are often expected to perform emotional labour, fulfilling roles as caregivers, nurturers, and emotional support systems for others. This societal expectation places undue emotional burden on young women, compelling them to prioritise the needs and emotions of others over their own wellbeing. The pressure to be emotionally available and resilient can contribute to feelings of exhaustion, burnout, and emotional distress. A study published in the Journal of Occupational Health Psychology found that women are more likely than men to engage in emotional labour, which is associated with increased levels of stress and emotional exhaustion.

Gender Stereotypes and Role Expectations

Traditional gender stereotypes perpetuate rigid role expectations for young women, prescribing limited roles and behaviours based on outdated notions of femininity. These stereotypes dictate how young women should dress, behave, and express themselves, constraining their autonomy and agency. The pressure to conform to gender norms and expectations can lead to internalised sexism, identity conflicts, and diminished self-esteem. According to a report by the American Psychological Association (APA), gender stereotypes can contribute to mental health issues such as depression, anxiety, and eating disorders among young women.

Social Comparison and FOMO

Social media platforms amplify feelings of social comparison and fear of missing out (FOMO) among young women, fuelling insecurities and self-doubt. The curated and idealised images presented on social media create unrealistic standards of success and happiness, leading young women to compare themselves unfavourably with others and experience feelings of inadequacy. Research published in the Journal of Abnormal Psychology found that excessive social media use is associated with increased levels of depression and anxiety among young adults.

In summary, societal expectations exert a significant influence on the mental health of young women, contributing to a myriad of challenges including body image concerns, academic pressures, emotional labor, gender stereotypes, and social comparison. Addressing these societal expectations requires a multifaceted approach that challenges ingrained norms, promotes diversity and inclusivity, and empowers young women to define success and happiness on their own terms. By fostering environments that celebrate authenticity, self-acceptance, and resilience, we can create a more supportive and nurturing society that prioritises mental health.

Addressing Loneliness, Social Media, and Peer Relationship

Loneliness has become a pervasive issue among young women, exacerbated by the rise of social media and evolving dynamics in peer relationships. Despite being more connected than ever through digital platforms, many young women experience feelings of isolation and disconnectedness.

Impact of Social Media on Peer Relationships

Social media platforms have transformed the landscape of peer relationships, offering new avenues for communication and connection. However, the curated nature of social media often leads to superficial interactions and a distorted perception of reality. Young women may feel pressured to present a polished and idealised version of themselves online, contributing to feelings of inadequacy and alienation when comparing their lives to others. Studies have shown that excessive use of social media is associated with increased feelings of loneliness and social isolation among young adults.

Peer Comparison

I'll never stop shouting from the rooftops about the dangers inherent in a society that constantly compares itself, not only to others but also to itself. I hear young women beating themselves up over what they used to look like, how they used to be carefree, and how they once feared nothing. It's bad enough when we see ourselves as inferior to our peers, but when we consider ourselves inferior versions of our younger self, we are in big trouble.

This year I'll celebrate my 56th birthday and I can't wait. For the past 30 years, I haven't thought of myself as getting older, I'm getting wiser. This year I'll celebrate being a year wiser, with another year's worth of experience to add to my life.

Young women may feel compelled to measure their worth and success based on the highlight reels of others, but we need to shake away feelings of envy, insecurity, and inadequacy.

Shifting Dynamics in Peer Relationships

The dynamics of peer relationships have evolved in the digital age, with virtual interactions often replacing face-to-face connections. While social media offers opportunities for maintaining friendships and expanding social networks, it can also hinder the development of meaningful, deep connections. Young women may struggle to navigate the complexities of online friendships, leading to a sense of disconnection and loneliness despite having a large number of online contacts. Research suggests that a lack of meaningful social connections is associated with increased risk of mental health issues such as depression and anxiety among young women.

Addressing Loneliness and Cultivating Authentic Connections
Recognising the detrimental effects of loneliness on mental health, efforts are being made to address this issue and foster authentic connections among young women. Mental health organisations, educational institutions, and community groups are implementing programs and initiatives aimed at reducing social isolation and promoting social connectedness. These initiatives may include peer support groups, mentorship programs, and community events designed to facilitate meaningful interactions and foster a sense of belonging.

Promoting Digital Wellbeing
To mitigate the negative impact of social media on peer relationships and mental health, initiatives promoting digital wellbeing are gaining traction. Digital literacy programs educate young women about healthy online behaviours, encouraging them to cultivate a balanced relationship with social media and prioritise real-life connections. Social media platforms are also implementing features to promote positive interactions and reduce harmful content, such as tools for managing screen time and algorithms that prioritise meaningful engagement over superficial metrics.

Building Resilience and Coping Strategies
Empowering young women with resilience and coping strategies is essential for navigating the challenges of loneliness and peer relationships. Psychoeducational interventions and workshops equip young women with skills for managing stress, building assertive communication skills, and cultivating self-esteem. These programs emphasise the importance of self-care, boundary-setting, and seeking support from trusted individuals in times of need.

In summary, addressing loneliness and fostering healthy peer relationships among young women requires a multifaceted approach that acknowledges the impact of social media, promotes digital wellbeing, and empowers us with resilience and coping strategies. By creating supportive environments that prioritise authentic connections and provide resources for building social skills and emotional resilience, we can mitigate the detrimental effects of loneliness and cultivate a sense of belonging and community among young women.

Empowering Young Women to Prioritise Their Mental Health

Accepting there is a problem—in any situation—is often a good strategy to finding a solution. Too often young women find themselves covering up the truth either by denial or from fear of exposing their vulnerabilities. Empowering young women to prioritise and seek support for their emotional mental health is crucial. Despite the increasing awareness surrounding mental health issues, societal stigma and cultural norms often deter young women from seeking help, exacerbating their struggles and perpetuating a cycle of silence and suffering.

Breaking the Stigma
One of the first steps in empowering young women to prioritise their mental health is breaking the stigma surrounding mental illness. Societal attitudes and misconceptions about mental health can create barriers to seeking support, leading young women to feel ashamed or embarrassed about their struggles. Education and awareness campaigns aimed at challenging stereotypes and normalising conversations about mental health are essential in dismantling stigma and fostering a culture of openness and acceptance.

Promoting Self-Care and Wellbeing
Empowering young women to prioritise their mental health involves promoting self-care practices and prioritising wellbeing. Encouraging young women to engage in activities that promote

relaxation, stress reduction, and emotional wellbeing, such as mindfulness exercises, creative expression, and physical activity, can help them build resilience and cope with life's challenges. Educating young women about the importance of self-care and providing them with resources and tools for managing stress and maintaining balance in their lives are key components of empowering them to take charge of their mental health.

Encouraging Help-Seeking Behaviours

Many young women may hesitate to seek help due to fear of judgment, concerns about confidentiality, or lack of knowledge about available resources. Providing education and information about mental health services, including counselling, therapy, support groups, and helplines, can empower young women to reach out for help when they need it. Normalising help-seeking behaviours and emphasising that seeking support is a sign of strength, not weakness, can reduce barriers to accessing mental health care.

Creating Supportive Environments

Creating supportive environments where young women feel safe, valued, and heard is essential for empowering them to prioritise and find support. Educational institutions, workplaces, and community organisations can play a crucial role in creating environments that promote mental health and wellbeing by implementing policies and programs that prioritise mental health, providing access to mental health resources and support services, and fostering a culture of empathy, understanding, and inclusivity.

Empowering Through Education and Advocacy

Empowering young women to prioritise their mental health also involves educating them about related issues, empowering them to advocate for their needs, and equipping them with the skills and knowledge to support others. Mental health literacy programs in schools and community settings can provide young women with information about common mental health conditions, coping strategies, and available resources, empowering them to recognise when they or others may need support and take appropriate action.

Why Mindcare Matters: Nurturing Your Inner Beauty

In today's crazy fast world, the pursuit of wellbeing extends far beyond surface-level beauty. Enter Mindcare—a revolutionary concept that transcends traditional self-care practices to nurture your inner beauty and transform your life from the inside out. At the forefront of this movement is HotChi, pioneering a new era of holistic wellness with its innovative Mindcare line. Here's why Mindcare matters and how HotChi's products can unleash your inner radiance:

Holistic Wellness: Mindcare recognises that true wellbeing encompasses every aspect of your being—mind, body, and spirit. By prioritising mental and emotional wellness, you embark on a journey of holistic healing and self-discovery. HotChi's Mindcare products are carefully crafted to nourish your entire being, supporting you on your path to wholeness.

Stress Relief and Resilience: If your day is filled with constant demands and pressures—and let's face it, whose isn't?—stress has become an unavoidable part of life. Mindcare offers effective strategies and tools to manage stress and build resilience. HotChi's Mindcare line includes calming meditation rituals, mood-boosting Aromatherapy blends, and stress-relief techniques designed to help you navigate life's challenges.

Enhanced Self-Awareness: Mindcare encourages introspection and self-reflection, fostering a deeper connection with your inner self. By practicing mindfulness and self-care rituals, you cultivate greater self-awareness and emotional intelligence. HotChi's Mindcare products serve as catalysts for self-discovery, empowering you to embrace your authentic self and live with purpose.

Empowerment and Confidence: Prioritising your mental and emotional wellbeing unlocks a newfound sense of empowerment and confidence. Mindcare rituals, such as affirmations and visualisation exercises, help you tap into your inner strength and unleash your full potential.

Sustainable Beauty: Mindcare promotes sustainable beauty that radiates from within. Unlike conventional beauty products that focus solely on external appearance, Mindcare nurtures your Chi, creating a lasting glow that transcends surface-level beauty. HotChi is committed to sustainability and ethical practices, ensuring that you can enhance your beauty guilt-free while supporting the planet.

In essence, Mindcare is not just a trend—it's a lifestyle that prioritises your *overall* wellbeing. Because when you nurture your mind, you unlock the true essence of beauty that lies within.

In conclusion, as young women navigating the complexities of modern life, it's crucial to recognise the unique challenges we face in safeguarding our mental wellbeing. The growing mental health crisis among us is influenced by various societal pressures, including unrealistic expectations, the omnipresence of social media, and the dynamics of peer relationships. However, amid these challenges lies an opportunity for empowerment and resilience.

It's imperative for us to prioritise our mental health and proactively seek support and resources when needed. By acknowledging and addressing societal norms and expectations that may contribute to our stress and anxiety, we can begin to reclaim control over our wellbeing. Cultivating supportive peer relationships built on trust, empathy, and understanding can provide invaluable sources of strength and encouragement.

Moreover, we must recognise the impact of social media on our mental health and take steps to manage our online presence mindfully. Setting boundaries, practicing digital detoxes, and engaging in self-care activities offline can help us strike a balance and protect our mental wellbeing in an increasingly digital world.

Ultimately, by prioritising our mental health, fostering supportive relationships, and embracing self-care practices, we empower ourselves to navigate the challenges of adolescence and young adulthood with resilience and grace. Together, we can break the stigma surrounding mental health and create a culture of openness, acceptance, and support where young women feel valued, heard, and empowered.

And with the innovative concept of Mindcare, we can further enhance our mental wellbeing and cultivate inner radiance that shines brightly in every aspect of our lives.

CHAPTER 4

PRACTICAL APPLICATIONS OF CHI

If I painted a bleak picture in the last chapter it's because you deserve to hear the truth. You may feel you're in control of your moods and emotions, and the term "mental health" is too strong to describe your mood swings, occasional irritability or lack of drive. You may think you just need a cuddle or a kick up the ass, but I'm here to give you a wake-up call and help in any way I can to protect you from what could become much worse.

I hear from teens and young women all the time that life is exhausting, boring, a let-down, yet a quick dose of Instagram or TikTok seems to take away the reality of an unfulfilled or stressful life, even if just for a moment. This is a normal reaction to distract ourselves from the mundane and it's been the same for generations but we need to self-moderate.

As a little kid, I remember the first thing my dad did when he got home from his office job was to switch off the family TV because my siblings and I were glued to it from the moment we got home from school. He said we'd end up with square eyes (maybe not such a bad thing for an Asian kid who was taunted for my looks at University!) Thankfully dad intervened and I don't have square eyes so I'm here to pass it forward and make sure you get as much practical advice as possible.

The following are practices you can include in your Chi journey. Start small and see how you get on.

Daily Practices for Cultivating Chi

Morning Rituals

Start your day with intentional morning rituals designed to awaken and energise your body, mind, and spirit. Begin by setting aside a few moments for deep breathing exercises, allowing oxygen to flow freely throughout your body and invigorate your cells. As you inhale deeply, envision the life-giving energy of Chi permeating every cell, revitalising your entire being. Combine Aromatherapy Essential Oils into your breathing ritual and you can expect to feel a heightened sense of wellbeing, calmness or energy, depending on which oils you choose.

Follow this with gentle stretching or yoga poses to release tension and increase flexibility, promoting Chi flow within your muscles and joints. As you move through each stretch, focus on the sensations in your body and the connection between breath and movement. Allow yourself to fully surrender to the present moment, embracing the flow of Chi as it moves through you.

Next, engage in mindfulness meditation to calm the mind and centre your thoughts for the day ahead. Find a comfortable seated position and close your eyes, bringing your awareness to your breath. Notice the sensation of air entering and leaving your nostrils, and allow your breath to naturally deepen and slow. As thoughts arise, gently redirect your attention back to your breath, cultivating a sense of inner stillness and presence.

Additionally, consider incorporating visualisation techniques into your morning routine, visualising positive outcomes and affirmations to set the tone for a productive and fulfilling day. Create a mental image of yourself embodying confidence, strength and vitality, and carry this vision with you throughout the day as a source of inspiration and motivation.

By starting your morning with these intentional practices, you lay the foundation for a harmonious and Chi-infused day. As you move through your morning rituals, remember that each breath, stretch, and moment of mindfulness is an opportunity to connect with the inherent power of Chi within you.

Mindful Movement

Throughout the day, prioritise mindful movement to keep Chi flowing smoothly within your body. This can include gentle exercises such as Tai Chi, Qi Gong, or yoga, which promote flexibility, balance, and Chi circulation. These practices combine slow, deliberate movements with conscious breathing, fostering a deep connection between mind, body, and spirit.

Incorporate short movement breaks into your daily routine, especially if you spend long hours sitting or working at a desk. Take a few minutes to stretch, walk, or practice simple Chi-enhancing movements to release tension and re-energise your body. As you move, pay attention to the sensations in your body and the rhythmic flow of your breath, allowing Chi to move freely and unimpeded throughout your entire being.

Conscious Breathing

Conscious breathing is a powerful tool for cultivating Chi and promoting relaxation and vitality. Throughout the day, take moments to pause and focus on your breath, inhaling deeply through your nose and exhaling slowly through your mouth. This rhythmic breathing pattern calms the nervous system, reduces stress, and enhances the flow of Chi within your body. Incorporate Aromatherapy oils into your daily breathwork for even greater results.

Practice mindful breathing during moments of stress or overwhelm to regain a sense of calm and composure. Close your eyes and bring your attention to your breath, allowing each inhale to fill you with peace and each exhale to release tension and negativity. As you breathe consciously, visualise the energy of Chi flowing freely throughout your body, revitalising your entire being and restoring balance within.

Energy Clearing Practices

Incorporate energy clearing practices into your daily routine to release stagnant Chi and promote energetic balance. This can include practices such as Acupressure and using Aromatherapy Essential Oils. The natural aromas will also purify your physical space and remove negative energy. You can also engage in visualisation exercises to visualise yourself surrounded by a protective shield of light, clearing away any energetic debris or disturbances.

Additionally, consider incorporating sound healing techniques such as chanting, singing bowls, or tuning forks to harmonise your energy field and promote Chi flow. These practices help to recalibrate your vibrational frequency and restore energetic balance.

In summary, by integrating these daily practices into your routine, you create a supportive environment for cultivating and maintaining a harmonious flow of Chi. Through intentional movement, conscious breathing, and energy clearing practices, you empower yourself to embrace the transformative power of Chi in your daily life. Each moment becomes an opportunity to connect with the inherent vitality of Chi, enhancing your overall wellbeing and deepening your connection to the universal life force that flows through you.

Chi in Physical Exercise and Movement

Physical exercise and movement play a crucial role in cultivating and maintaining the flow of Chi within the body. By engaging in mindful and intentional movement practices, you can enhance your vitality, promote Chi circulation, and support overall wellbeing. In this section, we will explore various forms of physical exercise and movement that are conducive to Chi cultivation.

Tai Chi

Tai Chi, also known as Tai Chi Chuan, is a centuries-old Chinese martial art that emphasises slow, deliberate movements and mindful breathing. Rooted in the principles of Yin and Yang and Traditional Chinese Medicine, Tai Chi promotes the balanced flow of Chi throughout the body, fostering physical, mental, and spiritual wellbeing.

Practitioners of Tai Chi perform a series of gentle, flowing movements, known as forms or sequences, with a focus on relaxation, coordination, and internal awareness. These movements are performed slowly and gracefully, allowing practitioners to cultivate Chi, or life energy, and harmonise the body's internal systems.

Tai Chi is particularly beneficial for improving balance, flexibility, and strength, making it suitable for individuals of all ages and fitness levels. Regular practice of Tai Chi can help reduce stress, enhance relaxation, and promote overall vitality, making it a valuable tool for cultivating Chi in daily life.

Qi Gong

Qi Gong, often referred to as "Chinese yoga", is an ancient Chinese practice that combines slow, flowing movements with deep breathing and mindfulness. Similar to Tai Chi, Qi Gong aims to promote the flow of Chi throughout the body, harmonising the body, mind, and spirit for optimal health.

Qi Gong exercises typically involve gentle, repetitive movements performed in a relaxed and focused manner. These movements are coordinated with deep, diaphragmatic breathing, allowing practitioners to cultivate and circulate Chi throughout the body's energy channels, or meridians.

There are many different styles and forms of Qi Gong, each with its own unique movements and techniques. Some forms of Qi Gong focus on specific health benefits, such as improving digestion, boosting immunity, or reducing stress, while others emphasise spiritual development and inner cultivation.

Regular practice of Qi Gong can help improve physical fitness, reduce tension and stress, and increase longevity. If proof were needed, my granddad who is 102 years old practices Qi Gong every day, usually with my granny who is 99 years old. They've been doing this every morning for as long as anyone can remember.

Yoga

Yoga is a holistic practice that combines physical postures, breathwork, and meditation. Originating in ancient India, Yoga has evolved into a popular form of exercise and mindfulness practice worldwide, with numerous styles and traditions.

Practitioners perform a series of "Asanas", or physical postures, designed to stretch, strengthen, and balance the body. These postures are coordinated with conscious breathing, allowing practitioners to cultivate awareness, focus, and presence in the moment.

Yoga is particularly effective for promoting flexibility, strength, and relaxation, making it an ideal practice for cultivating Chi and promoting overall wellbeing. By incorporating Yoga into your daily routine, you can enhance Chi circulation, reduce stress, and foster a deeper connection with your body and mind.

Martial Arts

Martial Arts encompass a wide range of traditional combat practices and disciplines, each with its own unique movements, techniques, and philosophies. While Martial Arts are often associated with physical combat and self-defence, they also offer profound benefits for cultivating Chi and promoting holistic wellbeing.

Many Martial Arts, such as Karate, Kung Fu, and Aikido, incorporate principles of Chi cultivation, mindfulness, and energy awareness into their training methods. Practitioners learn to harness their Chi to enhance their physical abilities, mental focus, and spiritual growth.

Through rigorous training, Martial Artists develop strength, agility, and discipline, as well as inner qualities such as resilience, courage, and compassion. By cultivating Chi through Martial Arts practice, individuals can enhance their vitality, promote balance and harmony, and foster personal growth and development.

In summary, incorporating physical exercise and movement practices such as Tai Chi, Qi Gong, Yoga, and Martial Arts into your daily routine can significantly enhance your Chi cultivation. These practices offer valuable tools for improving physical fitness, reducing stress, and fostering a deeper connection with your body, mind, and spirit.

Integrating Chi into Work and Daily Life

Begin each day with a mindful ritual to set Chi intentions that align with your goals and aspirations. This could involve starting the day with a short meditation or visualisation exercise to cultivate a positive mindset and clarify your intentions for the day ahead. By consciously directing your focus and energy towards positive outcomes, you set the stage for a more productive and fulfilling day.

Additionally, you can create a Chi intention journal where you write down your intentions and goals for the day, week, or month. This practice helps you stay focused and accountable, allowing you to track your progress and celebrate your achievements along the way.

Aromatherapy

Incorporating Aromatherapy into your daily beauty routine has enormous benefits to your wellbeing and mood. I have been doing this for years and it has transformed my life. Mix Essential Oils into your moisturiser and take a few deep breaths before massaging it into your face and neck as normal. The Essential Oils will give you a lift and make you smell great. Even better, check out the range of Chi-infused beauty products from HotChi for a great way to include Chi in your daily beauty or cleansing routine.

Mindful Movement Practices

Incorporate mindful movement practices into your daily routine to promote Chi flow and enhance your overall wellbeing. Activities such as Tai Chi, Qi Gong, or Yoga are excellent options as they combine gentle movement with breath awareness, helping to harmonise the body, mind, and spirit.

Alternatively, you can practice mindful walking as a form of moving meditation. Take time to walk in nature, paying attention to each step and the sensations in your body. Notice the rhythm of your breath and the sounds of your surroundings, allowing yourself to fully immerse in the present moment.

Whatever form of mindful movement you choose, make it a regular part of your routine to reap the benefits of increased vitality, improved circulation, and reduced stress levels.

Chi-Centric Workspaces

Create a Chi-centric workspace that supports focus, creativity, and productivity. Start by decluttering your workspace and organising it in a way that promotes flow and efficiency. Consider incorporating elements of nature, such as plants or natural light, to bring a sense of vitality and balance to your environment.

Pay attention to the ergonomics of your workspace, ensuring that your desk and chair are comfortable and conducive to good posture. Create designated areas for different tasks to minimise distractions and promote focus.

Additionally, infuse your workspace with positive energy by incorporating inspiring quotes, meaningful artwork, or personal mementos that uplift and motivate you. By creating a harmonious and Chi-enhancing environment, you set yourself up for success in your work.

Mindful Eating Practices

Adopt mindful eating practices to nourish your body and support Chi energy. Start by paying attention to the quality and source of your food, choosing whole, nutrient-rich foods that promote vitality and wellbeing. Aim to include a variety of colourful fruits and vegetables, whole grains, lean proteins, and healthy fats in your meals.

Practice mindful eating by slowing down and savouring each bite, chewing slowly to fully experience the flavours and textures of your food. Avoid distractions such as electronic devices or work-related tasks while eating, allowing yourself to focus solely on the act of nourishing your body.

Additionally, cultivate gratitude for the food on your plate and the nourishment it provides, fostering a deeper connection to the energy of the earth and the Chi within your body. By honouring your body with mindful eating practices, you support optimal digestion and energy levels.

Energy Management Techniques

Incorporate energy management techniques into your daily routine to maintain balance and prevent burnout. Start by scheduling regular breaks throughout the day to recharge and refocus your energy. Whether it's a short walk outside, a brief Meditation, or a few minutes of deep breathing, find activities that help you relax and restore your energy.

Practice progressive muscle relaxation by consciously tensing and then relaxing different muscle groups in your body, starting from your toes and working your way up to your head. This technique helps release tension and promotes relaxation, allowing Chi energy to flow more freely.

Additionally, practice deep breathing exercises to calm your mind and centre your energy. Try the 4-7-8 breathing technique, where you inhale for a count of four, hold your breath for a count of seven, and exhale for a count of eight. This simple yet powerful technique activates the body's relaxation response, promoting a sense of calm and wellbeing. See page 75 for step-by-step tutorials.

Chi in Relationships and Social Interactions

In relationships, Chi serves as a dynamic force that influences the quality of connections between individuals. It encompasses not only the physical and emotional aspects of interactions but also the energetic exchange that occurs on a deeper level. Understanding Chi in relationships involves recognising its subtle yet profound impact on the dynamics between partners, friends, family members, or colleagues.

At its core, Chi represents the flow of energy within and between individuals, shaping the nature of their relationships. This energy can be felt intuitively during interactions, influencing the level of comfort, resonance, and alignment between individuals. By acknowledging the presence of Chi in relationships, individuals can develop a deeper awareness of their connection with others and cultivate more authentic and fulfilling bonds.

Understanding Chi in relationships involves appreciating the interconnectedness of all living beings and recognising the ripple effects of our energetic interactions. Just as a stone dropped into a pond creates ripples that extend outward, our energetic exchanges with others have a ripple effect on the overall energy field of the relationship and beyond. By cultivating awareness of Chi in relationships, individuals can navigate their interactions with greater mindfulness, empathy, and compassion.

Balancing Chi in Social Interactions

Social interactions provide fertile ground for energetic exchange, as individuals come together in shared spaces and engage in communication, collaboration, and connection. Balancing Chi in social interactions involves maintaining equilibrium in the flow of energy between individuals to promote harmony, mutual respect and positive engagement.

This balance is essential for fostering healthy and harmonious relationships in various social contexts, including friendships, family gatherings, work environments, and community settings.

It requires individuals to be mindful of their own energy and how it interacts with the energies of others, ensuring that the exchange remains balanced and conducive to positive outcomes.

Techniques for balancing Chi in social interactions may include practices such as deep breathing, grounding exercises, and visualisation techniques. These practices help individuals centre themselves, cultivate presence, and remain attuned to the subtle cues and energetic dynamics at play during social interactions. By maintaining balance and harmony in their energetic exchanges, individuals can foster deeper connections, mutual understanding, and a sense of shared resonance with others.

Enhancing Communication with Chi

Effective communication lies at the heart of healthy and fulfilling relationships, and Chi can serve as a powerful catalyst for enhancing communication dynamics. Cultivating Chi awareness in communication involves developing a deeper understanding of the energetic aspects of communication and harnessing this awareness to enhance connection, clarity, and mutual understanding.

At its essence, Chi communication involves more than just the exchange of words—it encompasses the energetic nuances of tone, body language, and intention that accompany spoken communication. By cultivating mindfulness and presence in communication, individuals can sharpen their ability to listen deeply, express themselves authentically, and connect with others on a deeper level. It's also a sign of great leadership. Have you ever seen a teacher or a work boss keeping calm when things were going wrong.

They kept in control of the situation—never panicking or losing control—by not raising their voice or moving fast. That's Chi in action and you'll see it in all the great leaders. It comes across as confidence and it has an incredibly calming influence on everyone in the room.

Cultivating Chi in Relationship Dynamics

This involves fostering an environment where positive energy can thrive and flourish, nurturing qualities such as mutual respect, trust, and understanding. Building strong relationship dynamics requires intentional effort and commitment from both parties, as well as a willingness to cultivate Chi awareness and prioritise the flow of positive energy within the relationship.

Practices for cultivating Chi in relationship dynamics may include acts of kindness, emotional support, and open communication. These practices create a nurturing space for Chi to flow freely, fostering a sense of connection, harmony, and mutual wellbeing between partners. By prioritising the cultivation of Chi within the relationship, individuals can strengthen their bond, deepen their connection, and create a supportive and loving environment for growth and mutual fulfilment.

Aim to be that person in your social group or work team that is able to effortlessly alter the dynamics of a situation. Be the person that can walk into a busy room and instantly change the mood. Learn to understand how your positive Chi can have a calming effect and see how you can influence other's behaviour. That's the kind of social influencer you should aim to become.

As we conclude this chapter, it's evident that the practical applications of Chi extend far beyond mere theory—they offer tangible pathways to personal transformation and holistic wellbeing. By embracing daily practices to cultivate Chi, integrating it into physical exercise and work routines, and fostering Chi-centred relationships, we can experience profound shifts in our lives.

Through these practices, we not only enhance our vitality and resilience but also cultivate a deeper sense of harmony within ourselves and with the world around us.

CHAPTER 5

THE SCIENCE BEHIND AROMATHERAPY

There's no denying Aromatherapy's significant importance in Chi practices, from the therapeutic effects of Essential Oils on both body and mind to the volatile organic compounds that imbue Essential Oils with their distinctive scents and mood-enhancing properties, and the intricate interplay of neurotransmitters and hormones affected by Aromatherapy.

The Limbic System and Emotional Response

The limbic system is a complex network of structures in the brain that plays a crucial role in processing emotions, memories, and arousal. It encompasses several interconnected regions, including the amygdala, hippocampus, hypothalamus, and thalamus, which work together to regulate emotional responses and behaviour.

The Amygdala: Emotional Processing Centre

The amygdala is a small, almond-shaped structure located deep within the temporal lobe of the brain. It is renowned for its role in processing emotions, particularly fear and anxiety. However, the amygdala is also involved in the interpretation of other emotions, including happiness, sadness, and anger.

Aromatherapy has been shown to directly influence the amygdala's activity through the olfactory system. When we inhale aromatic compounds, such as those found in Essential Oils, they travel through the nasal passages and reach the olfactory bulb, which is connected to the amygdala. This direct pathway enables aromas to bypass conscious cognitive processing and evoke immediate emotional responses.

Research has demonstrated that certain Essential Oils, such as lavender and bergamot, can modulate amygdala activity, leading to changes in emotional states and behaviours. For example, lavender oil has been found to reduce anxiety levels by calming the amygdala's hyperactivity, while bergamot oil can uplift mood by enhancing amygdala activation associated with positive emotions.

By targeting the amygdala, Aromatherapy can effectively regulate emotional responses, alleviate stress, and promote emotional balance and wellbeing.

The Hippocampus: Memory Formation and Retrieval

The hippocampus is a vital brain structure located in the medial temporal lobe, adjacent to the amygdala. It plays a central role in memory formation and retrieval, particularly in the consolidation of new memories and the retrieval of past experiences.

Aromatherapy has been shown to influence hippocampal activity, particularly in the context of memory and learning. Certain aromatic compounds have been found to enhance cognitive function, improve memory retention, and facilitate learning processes by modulating hippocampal synaptic plasticity.

For example, studies have demonstrated that inhalation of rosemary Essential Oil can enhance memory performance and cognitive function by increasing hippocampal acetylcholine levels, a neurotransmitter involved in memory formation. Similarly, peppermint oil has been shown to improve cognitive performance and alertness by stimulating hippocampal activity.

By targeting the hippocampus, Aromatherapy can enhance cognitive function, improve memory consolidation, and support overall brain health and function.

The Hypothalamus: Regulation of Physiological Responses

The hypothalamus is a crucial brain structure located below the thalamus, responsible for regulating various physiological processes and maintaining homeostasis in the body. It serves as a central hub for coordinating the body's response to internal and external stimuli, including emotional and environmental stressors.

Aromatherapy has been shown to modulate hypothalamic activity, particularly in the context of stress and relaxation. Certain aromatic compounds have been found to influence hypothalamic-pituitary-adrenal (HPA) axis activity, leading to changes in stress hormone levels, autonomic nervous system function, and physiological responses.

For example, inhalation of lavender Essential Oil has been demonstrated to reduce cortisol levels, a key stress hormone, and modulate autonomic nervous system activity, leading to relaxation and stress reduction. Similarly, citrus Essential Oils, such as orange and lemon, have been shown to increase parasympathetic nervous system activity, promoting relaxation and reducing stress.

By targeting the hypothalamus and the HPA axis, Aromatherapy can effectively modulate stress responses, promote relaxation, and support overall physiological wellbeing.

The Thalamus: Relay Centre for Sensory Information

The Thalamus is a vital brain structure located deep within the forebrain, serving as a relay centre for transmitting sensory information to the cerebral cortex. It plays a crucial role in processing and integrating sensory inputs from the environment, including those related to smell and olfaction.

Aromatherapy can influence thalamic activity by modulating the transmission of sensory information to higher brain regions involved in emotional processing and perception. Inhalation of aromatic compounds can stimulate thalamic neurons, leading to enhanced sensory perception and emotional responses to aromas.

Research has shown that certain Essential Oils, such as peppermint and eucalyptus, can activate thalamic regions associated with alertness and cognitive arousal, leading to increased sensory awareness and mental clarity. Similarly, floral and citrus Essential Oils have been found to evoke positive emotional responses by enhancing thalamic processing of olfactory stimuli.

By targeting the thalamus, Aromatherapy can enhance sensory perception, evoke emotional responses, and promote cognitive arousal and alertness.

Understanding the intricate interplay between Aromatherapy and these key brain structures provides valuable insights into the mechanisms underlying the emotional and psychological effects of aromatic compounds. By targeting specific brain regions and neural pathways involved in emotional processing, memory formation, stress regulation, and sensory perception, Aromatherapy can effectively modulate mood, enhance cognitive function and alleviate stress.

Neurotransmitters and Brain Chemistry

Neurotransmitters are specialised chemical messengers that transmit signals between neurons (nerve cells) in the brain and nervous system. They play a crucial role in regulating various physiological and psychological functions, including mood, cognition, behaviour, and emotion.

Aromatherapy, through the inhalation or topical application of Essential Oils, can influence neurotransmitter activity in the brain, leading to changes in mood, cognition, and behaviour. Certain aromatic compounds found in Essential Oils have been shown to interact with neurotransmitter systems, modulating their release, uptake, and receptor activity.

Serotonin: The Mood-Stabilising Neurotransmitter

Serotonin, often referred to as the "happiness neurotransmitter," plays a key role in regulating mood, emotion, appetite, and sleep. It is involved in the modulation of various physiological processes and is crucial for emotional wellbeing and mental health.

Aromatherapy has been shown to affect serotonin levels in the brain. Certain Essential Oils, such as lavender, bergamot, and chamomile, contain bioactive compounds that can modulate serotonin synthesis, release, and receptor activity. Inhalation or topical application of these oils has been associated with mood enhancement, relaxation, and stress reduction, potentially through their interaction with the serotonergic system.

Dopamine: The Neurotransmitter of Reward and Pleasure

Dopamine is a neurotransmitter involved in the brain's reward pathway, playing a central role in motivation, pleasure, and reinforcement of behaviour. It is implicated in various functions, including motor control, cognition, mood regulation, and addiction.

Aromatherapy has been found to influence dopamine activity in the brain. Certain Essential Oils, such as citrus oils (e.g., orange, lemon) and peppermint, contain bioactive compounds that can modulate dopamine release, uptake, and receptor sensitivity. Inhalation or topical application of these oils promote feelings of pleasure, motivation, and reward, through their interaction with the dopaminergic system.

Gamma-Aminobutyric Acid (GABA): The Inhibitory Neurotransmitter

Gamma-aminobutyric acid (GABA) is the primary inhibitory neurotransmitter in the central nervous system, responsible for reducing neuronal excitability and promoting relaxation. It plays a crucial role in anxiety regulation, stress resilience, and sleep quality.

Aromatherapy has been shown to modulate GABAergic neurotransmission in the brain. Certain Essential Oils, such as lavender, chamomile, and sandalwood, contain bioactive compounds that can enhance GABA activity or mimic GABA's effects on receptor sites. Inhalation or topical application of these oils induce feelings of calmness, relaxation, and tranquility, through their interaction with the GABAergic system.

Endorphins: The Body's Natural Painkillers and Mood Enhancers

Endorphins are endogenous opioid peptides produced by the body in response to stress, pain, and physical exertion. They act as natural painkillers and mood enhancers, promoting feelings of euphoria, pleasure, and wellbeing.

Aromatherapy has been found to stimulate endorphin release in the brain. Certain Essential Oils, such as lavender, rosemary, and peppermint, contain bioactive compounds that can trigger endorphin release through their olfactory and pharmacological effects. Inhalation or topical application of these oils evoke feelings of comfort, relaxation, and happiness, through their interaction with the endorphin system.

By understanding the intricate interplay between Aromatherapy and neurotransmitters, we gain valuable insights into the mechanisms underlying the therapeutic effects of Essential Oils on mood, cognition, and emotional wellbeing. Aromatherapy offers a holistic approach to mental and emotional health, harnessing the power of nature to promote relaxation, reduce stress, and enhance overall wellbeing.

Essential Oils and Their Therapeutic Properties

The unique therapeutic properties of Aromatherapy as a potent healing method, and ability to promote overall wellbeing have long been revered. Through centuries of traditional use and modern scientific research, Aromatherapy Essential Oils have emerged as powerful allies in supporting physical, emotional, and mental health.

Some cheap oils are blended with artificial ingredients and fragrances, offering little to no benefits, so it is important that you use the best quality, certified and sustainable all-natural Essential Oils. Here are just a few from the hundreds available.

Lavender (Lavandula angustifolia)

Lavender Essential Oil is renowned for its calming and soothing properties. It has a sweet, floral aroma that promotes relaxation and alleviates stress and anxiety. Lavender oil is often used in Aromatherapy to induce feelings of calmness and improve sleep quality. Its analgesic and anti-inflammatory properties make it effective for relieving headaches, muscle tension, and minor skin irritations.

Peppermint (Mentha piperita)

Peppermint Essential Oil is known for its invigorating and refreshing scent. It has a cooling effect on the skin and can help alleviate headaches, migraines, and sinus congestion. Peppermint oil is also valued for its digestive benefits, helping to relieve nausea, indigestion, and bloating. Its energising aroma is often used to boost alertness and mental clarity.

Eucalyptus (Eucalyptus globulus)

Eucalyptus Essential Oil has a fresh, camphoraceous scent that is both uplifting and clarifying. It's commonly used to relieve respiratory congestion and promote clear breathing. Eucalyptus oil is often added to steam inhalations or diffusers to ease symptoms of colds, coughs, and sinus infections. Its antiseptic and antimicrobial properties make it beneficial for purifying the air and supporting immune health.

Tea Tree (Melaleuca alternifolia)

Tea tree Essential Oil is prized for its powerful antimicrobial and antiseptic properties. It has a fresh, medicinal aroma and is renowned for its ability to fight bacteria, viruses, and fungi. Tea tree oil is commonly used in skincare products to treat acne, blemishes, and fungal infections. Its purifying scent is also effective for clearing the air and promoting a clean, fresh environment.

Bergamot (Citrus bergamia)

Bergamot Essential Oil has a bright, citrusy scent that uplifts the mood and promotes emotional balance. It's often used to relieve stress, anxiety, and depression, helping to induce feelings of joy and optimism. Bergamot oil is also valued for its skincare benefits, particularly in treating oily or blemish-prone skin. Its refreshing aroma is a popular choice for promoting relaxation and wellbeing.

Chamomile (Matricaria chamomilla)

Chamomile Essential Oil has a sweet, floral aroma that is calming and comforting. It's renowned for its soothing effects on the mind and body, making it an ideal choice for promoting relaxation and restful sleep. Chamomile oil is often used in skincare products to soothe sensitive or irritated skin and is valued for its anti-inflammatory and healing properties.

Rosemary (Rosmarinus officinalis)
Rosemary Essential Oil has a fresh, herbaceous scent that is invigorating and stimulating. It's known for its clarifying and uplifting effects on the mind, helping to improve focus, concentration, and mental alertness. Rosemary oil is often used in hair care products to promote healthy hair growth and scalp health. Its energising aroma is also valued for promoting feelings of vitality and wellbeing.

Ylang Ylang (Cananga odorata)
Ylang ylang Essential Oil has a sweet, floral aroma that is both exotic and sensual. It's known for its calming and aphrodisiac properties, making it an ideal choice for promoting relaxation and intimacy. Ylang ylang oil is often used in Aromatherapy to reduce stress, anxiety, and tension, while also uplifting the mood and enhancing sensuality.

Lemon (Citrus limon)
Lemon Essential Oil has a bright, citrusy aroma that is refreshing and uplifting. It's prized for its cleansing and purifying properties, making it an ideal choice for promoting a clean, fresh environment. Lemon oil is often used in natural cleaning products to disinfect surfaces and neutralise odours. Its invigorating scent is also effective for boosting mood and energy levels.

Sandalwood (Santalum album)
Sandalwood Essential Oil has a rich, woody aroma that is grounding and calming. It's revered for its ability to promote relaxation, reduce stress, and enhance mental clarity. Sandalwood oil is often used in meditation and spiritual practices to create a sense of inner peace and tranquility. Its soothing scent is also valued for promoting emotional balance and wellbeing.

Frankincense (Boswellia carterii)
Frankincense Essential Oil has a warm, resinous aroma that is both uplifting and grounding. It's loved for its spiritual and therapeutic properties, making it a popular choice for meditation and prayer. Frankincense oil is often used in skincare products to

promote cellular regeneration and reduce the appearance of fine lines and wrinkles. Its calming scent is also effective for reducing stress and promoting relaxation.

Patchouli (Pogostemon cablin)
Patchouli Essential Oil has a rich, earthy aroma that is grounding and balancing. It's known for its antidepressant and aphrodisiac properties, making it a popular choice for promoting emotional wellbeing and intimacy. Patchouli oil is often used in skincare products to promote healthy skin and reduce the appearance of wrinkles and scars.

Geranium (Pelargonium graveolens)
Geranium Essential Oil has a floral, rosy aroma that is uplifting and balancing. It's valued for its calming and antidepressant properties, making it an ideal choice for promoting emotional balance and relaxation. Geranium oil is often used in skincare products to promote healthy, glowing skin and reduce inflammation and irritation.

Neroli (Citrus aurantium)
Neroli Essential Oil has a sweet, floral aroma that is uplifting and calming. It's valued for its antidepressant and aphrodisiac properties, making it an ideal choice for promoting emotional wellbeing and intimacy. Neroli oil is often used in skincare products to promote healthy, glowing skin and reduce inflammation and irritation.

Cedarwood (Juniperus virginiana)
Cedarwood Essential Oil has a warm, woody aroma that is grounding and calming. It's known for its sedative and aphrodisiac properties, making it a popular choice for promoting relaxation and intimacy. Cedarwood oil is often used in Aromatherapy to reduce stress, anxiety, and tension, while also promoting restful sleep.

Juniper Berry (Juniperus communis)
Juniper berry Essential Oil has a fresh, woody aroma that is invigorating and uplifting. It's known for its detoxifying and purifying properties, making it an ideal choice for promoting emotional wellbeing and physical health. Juniper berry oil is often used in skincare products to promote healthy, clear skin and reduce inflammation and irritation.

Rose (Rosa damascena)
Rose Essential Oil has a rich, floral aroma that is uplifting and comforting. It's prized for its antidepressant and aphrodisiac properties, making it an ideal choice for promoting emotional wellbeing and intimacy. Rose oil is often used in skincare products to promote healthy, glowing skin and reduce inflammation and irritation.

Cinnamon Bark (Cinnamomum zeylanicum)
Cinnamon bark Essential Oil has a warm, spicy aroma that is invigorating and stimulating. It's valued for its energising and aphrodisiac properties, making it a popular choice for promoting vitality and intimacy. Cinnamon bark oil is often used in Aromatherapy to reduce fatigue, enhance mental clarity, and improve mood.

Grapefruit (Citrus paradisi)
Grapefruit Essential Oil has a fresh, citrusy aroma that is uplifting and energising. It's known for its antidepressant and detoxifying properties, making it an ideal choice for promoting emotional wellbeing and physical health. Grapefruit oil is often used in skincare products to promote healthy, clear skin and reduce inflammation and irritation.

In conclusion, the intricate relationship between Aromatherapy and the human brain underscores the profound impact of scent on our emotional and physical wellbeing. Through the limbic system, aromas interact with our emotions, memories, and stress responses, offering a direct pathway to influence our mood and overall mental state.

Moreover, the modulation of neurotransmitters and brain chemistry by Essential Oils highlights their therapeutic potential in alleviating various mental health conditions, such as anxiety and depression. By understanding the science behind Aromatherapy, particularly the role of the limbic system and neurotransmitters, we gain insight into harnessing the power of scent for holistic wellness.

Additionally, exploring the diverse therapeutic properties of Essential Oils underscores their versatility in addressing a wide range of physical and emotional ailments, promoting balance and harmony within the body and mind. Through continued research and exploration, we can further unlock the potential of Aromatherapy as a valuable tool for enhancing overall emotional and mental health.

CHAPTER 6

BREATHWORK AND CHI ACTIVATION

Breathwork, the intentional control and manipulation of the breath, has been practiced for centuries across various cultures and traditions as a means of promoting overall wellbeing and inner harmony. Through conscious breathing techniques, we can tap into the profound connection between the breath, the mind, and our emotional state, facilitating a deeper understanding of ourselves and fostering greater emotional resilience.

In this section, we explore the profound role of breath in activating and harmonising our life force-giving Chi. Breath serves as the bridge between our physical body and energetic essence, facilitating the exchange of vital oxygen and Chi throughout our entire being. By understanding the intricate relationship between breath and Chi, we can unlock the transformative power of conscious breathing practices to optimise our energy flow and enhance our overall wellbeing.

The Role of Breath in Chi Activation

Breath serves as the vital link between our physical and energetic bodies, facilitating the exchange of oxygen and Chi throughout our system. This dynamic interplay between breath and Chi ensures the nourishment and vitality of every cell and organ in our body. By understanding the profound connection between our breath patterns and energetic flow, we can harness the power of breath to optimise Chi activation.

Mindful Breathing for Chi Alignment

Mindful breathing is a foundational practice for aligning with our Chi and cultivating inner harmony. It involves bringing conscious awareness to each inhalation and exhalation, anchoring our attention in the present moment. By observing the rhythm of our breath, we can synchronise our inner and outer worlds, fostering a sense of centredness and balance. Mindful breathing serves as a gateway to accessing the deeper dimensions of our being, where the essence of Chi resides.

Breathwork Techniques for Chi Circulation

Various breathwork techniques offer powerful tools for regulating and enhancing Chi circulation throughout the body. Practices such as pranayama, originating from yoga traditions, and Qi Gong breathing exercises, rooted in Traditional Chinese Medicine, provide time-tested methods for optimising Chi flow. These techniques often involve specific patterns of breathing, such as deep belly breathing or alternate nostril breathing, combined with breath retention and visualisation exercises. By incorporating breathwork into our daily routine, we can tap into the transformative potential of Chi activation.

Quality of Breath and Chi Vitality

The quality of our breath profoundly influences the quality of our Chi. Shallow, constricted breathing patterns restrict the flow of Chi and contribute to energetic stagnation and imbalance. In contrast, deep, diaphragmatic breathing promotes expansive Chi circulation and vitality throughout the body. By cultivating a practice of deep, conscious breathing, we can nourish and revitalise our Chi, fostering a state of vibrant health and wellbeing.

Unlocking Potential Through Breath Mastery

Mastery of breathwork is key to unlocking the full potential of Chi activation and empowerment. By honing our breath awareness and integrating breathwork techniques into our daily lives, we can awaken the latent vitality and resilience of our life force energy. Breath becomes a gateway to expanded consciousness, inner peace, and profound transformation. Through dedicated practice and mindful engagement with our breath, we embark on a journey of self-discovery and Chi activation, embracing the boundless possibilities of our inherent vitality.

Techniques for Conscious Breathing

Now we will explore various techniques for conscious breathing, each designed to harness the power of breath to activate and balance our Chi. Through mindful awareness and intentional breathwork, we can tap into the inherent wisdom of our respiratory system to promote relaxation, vitality, and inner harmony. Here are practical methods for cultivating a deeper connection with our breath and Chi energy.

Diaphragmatic Breathing

Also known as deep belly breathing, this technique involves inhaling deeply through the nose, allowing the diaphragm to fully expand and fill the lungs with air. Exhale slowly through the mouth, emptying the lungs completely as the diaphragm contracts.

Box Breathing

This technique involves inhaling slowly and deeply for a count of four, holding the breath for a count of four, exhaling slowly and completely for a count of four, and then holding the breath out for a count of four before starting the cycle again.

Alternate Nostril Breathing (Nadi Shodhana)

This yogic breathing technique involves using the thumb and ring finger to alternately close off one nostril while inhaling and exhaling through the other nostril. This practice is believed to balance the flow of energy in the body and calm the mind.

Sama Vritti (Equal Breathing)

With this technique, you inhale and exhale for an equal count, such as inhaling for a count of four and exhaling for a count of four. This rhythmic breathing pattern can help synchronise the breath with the heartbeat and promote relaxation.

4-7-8 Breathing

This technique involves inhaling deeply through the nose for a count of four, holding the breath for a count of seven, and exhaling slowly through the mouth for a count of eight. It is believed to promote relaxation and reduce stress.

These techniques can be adapted and combined based on individual preferences and needs. They serve as valuable tools for enhancing mindfulness, reducing stress, and cultivating a deeper connection with the breath and Chi energy.

Breathwork Practices for Energy and Relaxation

Next we'll explore various breathwork practices aimed at both boosting energy and inducing relaxation. These practices tap into the power of the breath to influence our physiological and mental states, promoting a sense of balance and wellbeing.

Let's break down each breathwork practice into simple, step-by-step instructions for easy execution. With each of these practices, sit comfortably or lie down with your spine straight and shoulders relaxed.

Kapalabhati (Skull Shining Breath)

This yogic breathing technique involves rapid and forceful exhalations through the nose, followed by passive inhalations. It is believed to clear the mind, increase alertness, and invigorate the body by stimulating the nervous system.

1. Take a deep breath in through your nose, filling your lungs with air.

2. Exhale forcefully and quickly through your nose, contracting your abdominal muscles to push the air out.

3. Allow the inhalation to happen naturally without force. Focus on the sharp exhalations, aiming for a rhythmic pace.

4. Start with a slower pace and gradually increase the speed as you become more comfortable.

5. Practice for 1-3 minutes to begin with, gradually extending the duration as you progress.

Ujjayi Breath (Victorious Breath)

Ujjayi breath is characterised by a slight constriction of the throat during both inhalation and exhalation, creating a soft hissing sound resembling ocean waves. This rhythmic breathing technique promotes relaxation, focus, and mental clarity.

1. Take a deep breath in through your nose, filling your lungs completely.

2. Constrict the back of your throat slightly as you exhale through your nose, creating a soft hissing or ocean-like sound.

3. Keep the inhalation and exhalation equal in duration, focusing on the sound and sensation of the breath.

4. Practice for 5-10 minutes, gradually extending the duration as you become more accustomed to the technique.

Bhastrika (Bellows Breath)

Bhastrika involves rapid and forceful inhalations and exhalations through the nose, emphasising the movement of the diaphragm. This dynamic breathwork practice increases oxygenation in the body, boosts energy levels, and revitalises the mind.

1. Take a deep breath in through your nose, filling your lungs with air.

2. Exhale forcefully and rapidly through your nose, emphasising the movement of your diaphragm.

3. Inhale quickly and forcefully, allowing your abdomen to expand fully.

4. Continue this rapid, forceful breathing pattern, keeping the pace steady and controlled.

5. Practice for 1-3 minutes initially, gradually increasing the duration as you build stamina and comfort with the technique.

Alternate Nostril Breathing (Nadi Shodhana)

As mentioned earlier, alternate nostril breathing is a balancing breathwork practice that involves alternating between breathing through the left and right nostrils. This technique helps synchronise the left and right hemispheres of the brain, promoting mental balance and relaxation.

1. Use your right thumb to close your right nostril and inhale deeply through your left nostril.

2. Close your left nostril with your right ring finger, and exhale completely through your right nostril.

3. Inhale deeply through your right nostril, then close it with your right thumb.

4. Open your left nostril and exhale completely through it.

5. *This completes one cycle. Continue alternating nostrils for several rounds, maintaining a slow and steady pace.*

6. *Practice for 5-10 minutes, gradually increasing the duration as you become more familiar with the technique.*

Breath of Fire (Kapalabhati Variation)

This rapid and rhythmic breathwork practice involves quick and forceful exhalations through the nose, followed by passive inhalations. Breath of Fire is believed to increase vitality, mental clarity, and emotional balance.

1. *Take a deep breath in through your nose, filling your lungs with air.*

2. *Exhale forcefully and rapidly through your nose, allowing your abdomen to contract with each exhalation.*

3. *Inhale passively through your nose, allowing the inhalation to happen naturally without force.*

4. *Focus on the rapid and rhythmic exhalations, aiming for a steady pace.*

5. *Practice for 1-3 minutes initially, gradually increasing the duration as you build stamina and comfort with the technique.*

These breathwork practices can be incorporated into daily routines to cultivate energy, reduce stress, and enhance overall wellbeing. Experiment with different techniques to find those that resonate most with you, and practice them regularly to harness the transformative power of the breath.

Breathwork for Emotional Balance and Mental Clarity

Let's now look into the transformative power of breathwork for cultivating emotional balance and enhancing mental clarity. From simple techniques that soothe the nervous system to more dynamic practices that invigorate the body and mind, each exercise offers a unique pathway to cultivating inner calm and enhancing cognitive function. Whether you're seeking relief from stress and anxiety or striving to sharpen your focus and concentration, the practices outlined here provide valuable tools for navigating life's challenges with greater ease and clarity.

Each breathing technique targets specific areas of wellbeing and offers unique benefits. Let's explore how each technique contributes to emotional balance, stress reduction, and mental clarity.

Box Breathing (Square Breathing)

Targets: Stress Reduction, Emotional Regulation

Benefits: Box breathing is a powerful technique for reducing stress and promoting emotional balance. By equalising the length of each breath and incorporating brief pauses between inhalation and exhalation, this practice activates the body's relaxation response. It helps regulate the autonomic nervous system, leading to a sense of calm and centredness. Box breathing also encourages mindfulness and present-moment awareness, making it an effective tool for managing anxiety and promoting emotional resilience.

1. *Sit comfortably with your spine straight and shoulders relaxed.*

2. *Inhale deeply through your nose for a count of four, allowing your abdomen to expand.*

3. *Hold your breath at the top of the inhale for a count of four.*

4. *Exhale slowly and completely through your nose or mouth for a count of four, emptying your lungs.*

5. *Hold your breath at the bottom of the exhale for a count of four.*

6. *Repeat this cycle for several rounds, focusing on the rhythm of your breath and the sensation of expansion and release.*

Three-Part Breath (Dirga Pranayama)

Targets: Emotional Regulation, Relaxation

Benefits: The three-part breath is a foundational practice in yoga and pranayama, known for its calming and grounding effects. By consciously directing the breath into three distinct areas of the torso—the abdomen, ribcage, and chest—this technique promotes deep relaxation and emotional balance. It enhances oxygenation of the body, leading to improved circulation and reduced tension. The three-part breath also encourages a sense of inner spaciousness and ease, making it an ideal practice for stress relief and emotional resilience.

1. Begin by sitting or lying down in a comfortable position.

2. Place one hand on your abdomen and the other on your chest.

3. Inhale deeply through your nose, directing the breath into your abdomen first, then filling your ribcage, and finally allowing your chest to expand.

4. Exhale slowly and completely through your nose, reversing the process by emptying your chest, ribcage, and abdomen.

5. Continue this three-part breathing pattern for several rounds, focusing on the smooth flow of breath through each part of your torso.

Lion's Breath (Simhasana Pranayama)

Target: Stress Relief, Release of Tension

Benefits: Lion's breath is an energising and cathartic breathwork practice that releases tension and invigorates the body and mind. By incorporating forceful exhalation through the mouth and vocalising a roaring sound, this technique helps release pent-up emotions and stress. Lion's breath activates the diaphragm and facial muscles, promoting a sense of lightness and openness. It encourages a playful attitude and fosters a sense of empowerment, making it an effective practice for releasing stress and enhancing vitality.

1. Come into a comfortable seated position with your knees bent and your hands resting on your thighs.

2. Inhale deeply through your nose, filling your lungs with air.

3. Exhale forcefully through your mouth, sticking out your tongue and roaring like a lion.

4. As you exhale, open your mouth wide, stretch your tongue out toward your chin, and make a "ha" sound, releasing any tension in your face and throat.

5. Repeat this breath several times, allowing yourself to let go of stress and tension with each exhale.

Humming Bee Breath (Bhramari Pranayama)
Target: Stress Reduction, Mental Clarity
Benefits: Humming bee breath is a soothing and meditative practice that calms the mind and nervous system. By producing a gentle humming sound on the exhale, this technique activates the vagus nerve, which helps regulate stress and promote relaxation. The vibrations created by the humming sound resonate in the head and throat, producing a calming effect on the mind and body. Humming bee breath reduces mental chatter and promotes inner stillness, making it an effective practice for enhancing mental clarity and focus.

1. Find a comfortable seated position with your spine straight and your hands resting on your knees.

2. Close your eyes and take a deep breath in through your nose.

3. As you exhale, make a soft humming sound like a bee, keeping your lips gently closed and your teeth slightly apart.

4. Feel the vibration of the sound resonating in your head and throat.

5. *Continue to hum on the exhale for as long as comfortable, focusing on the soothing and calming effect of the sound.*

6. *Repeat this practice for several rounds, allowing each exhale to deepen your sense of relaxation and mental clarity.*

4-7-8 Breathing

Target: Relaxation, Sleep Quality

Benefits: 4-7-8 breathing is a simple yet potent technique for inducing relaxation and promoting restful sleep. By extending the exhalation and incorporating a brief breath hold, this practice stimulates the body's parasympathetic nervous system, which is responsible for rest and digestion. 4-7-8 breathing promotes a sense of deep relaxation and tranquility, making it an ideal practice for reducing stress and improving sleep quality. It calms the mind and prepares the body for rest, facilitating a smooth transition into sleep.

1. *Sit or lie down in a comfortable position, allowing your body to relax.*

2. *Close your eyes and take a deep breath in through your nose for a count of four.*

3. *Hold your breath for a count of seven.*

4. *Exhale slowly and completely through your mouth for a count of eight, making a whooshing sound as you release the breath.*

5. *Repeat this cycle for four full breaths, focusing on the calming rhythm of the 4-7-8 pattern.*

6. *As you practice, allow your mind to become quiet and still, letting go of any tension or distractions.*

These breathwork exercises can be incorporated into your daily routine to promote emotional balance, reduce stress, and enhance mental clarity. Experiment with each practice and find what works best for you, adjusting the duration and intensity to suit your needs.

With regular practice, you'll discover the transformative power of breathwork in supporting your overall wellbeing.

In conclusion, breathwork serves as a powerful gateway to activating and harmonising the flow of Chi within the body. Through conscious engagement with the breath, we can unlock the transformative potential of Chi, fostering greater energy, relaxation, emotional balance, and mental clarity. By integrating these breathwork practices into our daily lives, we cultivate a deeper connection to our inner vitality and resilience, empowering us to navigate life's challenges with grace and ease. As we continue to explore the intricate interplay between breath, Chi, and overall wellbeing, may we harness the inherent wisdom of our breath to cultivate a life of balance, vitality, and inner harmony.

CHAPTER 7

ACUPRESSURE AND MERIDIANS

In the intricate tapestry of Traditional Chinese Medicine, the concept of Chi meridians and energy channels stands as a testament to the profound interconnectedness of the human body, mind, and spirit. According to ancient Chinese philosophy, the body is traversed by a network of meridians—subtle pathways through which our Chi flows incessantly, nourishing and sustaining every cell, tissue, and organ. These meridians are akin to rivers of energy, linking various physiological and psychological aspects of human existence.

Understanding Chi Meridians and Energy Channels

Chi meridians are not merely physical pathways; they embody the holistic understanding of health and wellness in Traditional Chinese Medicine, encompassing the dynamic interplay between the physical, emotional, and spiritual dimensions of human experience. Each meridian corresponds to specific organs and organ systems, as well as emotional and psychological attributes, reflecting the intricate web of connections between internal and external factors influencing overall wellbeing.

In Traditional Chinese Medicine theory, the flow of Chi along the meridians is believed to be vital for maintaining balance and harmony within the body. When Chi becomes stagnant or imbalanced, it can lead to disharmony and eventually manifest as physical or emotional ailments. By understanding the intricate pathways of Chi meridians and energy channels, practitioners of Traditional Chinese Medicine aim to identify and address imbalances in the flow of Chi, thereby restoring health and vitality to the individual.

Moreover, the concept of Chi meridians transcends the physical realm, extending into the realms of consciousness and spirituality. In addition to facilitating the flow of vital energy within the body, meridians are believed to serve as conduits for the transmission of consciousness and spiritual insights, fostering a deeper connection with the universal life force.

Overall, the understanding of Chi meridians and energy channels in Traditional Chinese Medicine offers a holistic framework for comprehending the dynamic interplay between the physical, emotional, and spiritual dimensions of human health. By delving into the profound wisdom of Chi meridians, we embark on a journey of self-discovery and healing, unlocking the innate potential for balance, harmony, and vitality within ourselves.

Self Acupressure Points for Balancing Chi

Acupressure is another ancient healing art rooted in Traditional Chinese Medicine. It is a therapeutic technique that involves applying pressure to specific points on the body to stimulate the flow of Chi and promote healing. Similar to Acupuncture but without the use of needles, Acupressure targets key energy points along the body's meridians to restore balance and alleviate various physical and emotional ailments.

Acupressure points, also known as acupoints or pressure points, are specific locations on the body where Chi energy is concentrated and accessible for manipulation. These points are typically found along the body's meridians, which are the pathways through which Chi flows. By applying gentle pressure or massage to these points yourself, you are able to restore the smooth and balanced flow of Chi.

There are hundreds of Acupressure points located throughout the body, each with its unique therapeutic properties and functions.

When massaging these Acupressure points, it's essential to listen to your body and adjust the pressure according to your comfort level. Start with gentle pressure and gradually increase it as needed, but always avoid applying excessive force. Additionally, remember to take slow, deep breaths during the massage to enhance relaxation and promote the flow of Chi energy.

Hegu (LI4)

Located on the back of the hand between the thumb and index finger, Hegu is renowned for its ability to relieve pain, reduce stress, and promote overall relaxation.

1. Find the fleshy webbing between your thumb and index finger.

2. Using your opposite thumb and index finger, apply firm pressure to the area, gradually increasing the intensity.

3. Hold the pressure for 1-2 minutes while taking slow, deep breaths.

4. Release the pressure and repeat on the other hand if desired.

Zusanli (ST36)

Situated on the lower leg below the kneecap, Zusanli is revered for its revitalising and immune-boosting effects, making it a popular choice for enhancing overall vitality and wellbeing.

1. Locate the point on your lower leg, about four finger-widths below the kneecap and one finger-width towards the outside of the leg.

2. Using your thumb or fingers, apply firm pressure to the point, using a circular or kneading motion.

3. Maintain the pressure for 1-2 minutes, breathing deeply and focusing on relaxation.

4. Release the pressure and switch to the other leg if desired.

Neiguan (PC6)

Found on the inner forearm, Neiguan is renowned for its ability to alleviate nausea, calm the mind, and soothe emotional distress, making it an invaluable point for managing stress and anxiety.

1. Find the point on your inner forearm, approximately two finger-widths above the wrist crease.

2. Use your thumb or fingers to apply gentle pressure to the point, gradually increasing the intensity.

3. Massage the area in a circular or up-and-down motion for 1-2 minutes, focusing on relaxation and stress relief.

4. Repeat on the other arm if desired.

Baihui (GV20)

Positioned at the top of the head, Baihui is celebrated for its capacity to clear the mind, enhance mental clarity, and promote spiritual connection, making it an excellent point for promoting overall balance and harmony.

1. Locate the point at the top of your head, along the midline.

2. Use your fingertips to apply gentle pressure to the area, using a circular or tapping motion.

3. Massage the point for 1-2 minutes while taking slow, deep breaths and focusing on mental clarity and relaxation.

4. You can also gently massage the area with your fingertips in a clockwise or counterclockwise direction.

Yongquan (KI1)

Located on the sole of the foot, Yongquan is revered for its grounding and centring effects, making it an ideal point for promoting relaxation, reducing anxiety, and restoring emotional equilibrium.

1. Find the point on the sole of your foot, between the second and third toes.

2. Use your thumb or fingers to apply firm pressure to the area, using a circular or kneading motion.

3. Maintain the pressure for 1-2 minutes, breathing deeply and focusing on grounding and relaxation.

4. Switch to the other foot and repeat the massage if desired.

These are just a few examples of the myriad Acupressure points that exist throughout the body, each offering unique benefits and therapeutic effects. By harnessing the power of Acupressure and targeting specific pressure points, you can tap into the body's innate healing potential, restore balance to your energy system, and cultivate a profound sense of wellbeing.

Integrating Acupressure into Daily Self-Care Routines

Daily practice of Acupressure is a powerful way to promote overall wellbeing and balance the flow of Chi energy in the body. Here's how you can incorporate Acupressure into your daily routine.

My Tip: Apply Aromatherapy Essential Oils to your fingers for an even more effective Acupressure routine. The Aromatherapy will boost your mood and the Essential Oils will be absorbed into your skin. Just remember to dilute the Essential Oil as it could burn your skin. Add a few drops to your moisturiser or better still, use an all-natural facial oil from HotChi's Mindcare range.

Morning Routine
Start your day with a few minutes of Acupressure to awaken your body and mind. Focus on stimulating Acupressure points related to energy and vitality, such as Hegu (LI4) on the hands or Zusanli (ST36) on the legs. This can help increase circulation, boost energy

levels, and enhance mental clarity to prepare you for the day ahead.

Midday Break

Take a short break during the day to relieve stress and tension with Acupressure. Focus on points like Neiguan (PC6) on the inner forearm or Baihui (GV20) on the top of the head to promote relaxation, reduce anxiety, and improve focus. Spend a few minutes massaging these points to release built-up tension and reset your energy.

Evening Relaxation

Wind down in the evening with a calming Acupressure routine to promote relaxation and prepare for restful sleep. Focus on points like Yongquan (KI1) on the soles of the feet or Yintang (EX-HN3) between the eyebrows to soothe the mind and body, relieve fatigue, and promote deep relaxation. Spend a few minutes massaging these points before bedtime to help you unwind and enjoy a peaceful night's sleep.

Self-Care Rituals

Incorporate Acupressure into your self-care rituals, such as skincare routines or meditation practices. Pairing Acupressure with facial massage techniques can enhance the absorption of skincare products, promote lymphatic drainage, and rejuvenate the skin. You can also combine Acupressure with meditation by focusing on specific points to deepen relaxation, release tension, and enhance mindfulness.

Daily Check-In

Use Acupressure as a tool for daily self-care and self-awareness. Take a few moments throughout the day to check in with yourself and identify areas of tension or discomfort in your body. Use Acupressure to target these areas and release tension, promoting a sense of balance and wellbeing. By incorporating Acupressure into your daily routine, you can cultivate a deeper connection with your body, mind, and Chi energy, promoting overall health and vitality.

By integrating Acupressure into your daily self-care routine, you can support the free flow of Chi energy in the body, enhance relaxation, and promote overall wellbeing. Experiment with different Acupressure points and techniques to find what works best for you, and enjoy the benefits of this ancient healing practice in your daily life.

In conclusion, this chapter has provided a comprehensive exploration of the ancient practice of Acupressure and its profound connection to the balance of Chi energy within the body. Through understanding the intricate network of Chi meridians and energy channels, you gain insight into the vital pathways through which life force energy flows, influencing physical, emotional, and mental wellbeing.

Moreover, the integration of Acupressure—and Aromatherapy Essential Oils—into daily self-care routines empowers us to take an active role in nurturing our health and vitality. Whether incorporated into morning rituals, midday breaks, or evening relaxation practices, Acupressure offers a gentle yet effective way to balance, harmony, and resilience in everyday life.

CHAPTER 8

MEDITATION AND INNER HARMONY

Let's immerse ourselves in the serene world of Meditation and Inner Harmony. In this chapter, we explore the profound practice of meditation and its remarkable capacity to cultivate inner peace, emotional balance, and spiritual connection.

Introduction to Meditation for Chi Cultivation

Meditation serves as a bridge between the physical and spiritual realms, providing a space for introspection, self-awareness, and energetic alignment. By quieting the mind and turning our focus inward, we can tap into the abundant reservoir of Chi that flows through our being, replenishing our vitality and restoring balance to the body, mind, and spirit.

Throughout history, many meditation traditions have emerged, each offering unique techniques and approaches for cultivating Chi. From mindfulness meditation to guided visualisation and breathwork practices, the methods of meditation are diverse yet interconnected in their shared goal of awakening the latent potential of Chi within us.

In this section, we'll explore the fundamental principles of meditation, including posture, breath awareness, and mental focus.

By establishing a solid foundation in meditation, we lay the groundwork for deepening our connection to Chi, fostering inner harmony, and unlocking the limitless possibilities of our true essence.

Mindfulness Meditation Practices

Mindfulness meditation is a form of meditation that emphasises present moment awareness and non-judgmental observation of thoughts, feelings, and sensations. In this section, we will explore various mindfulness meditation practices that are designed to cultivate a heightened sense of awareness and promote inner harmony.

Breath Awareness

One of the foundational practices in mindfulness meditation is breath awareness. By bringing attention to the natural rhythm of the breath, practitioners learn to anchor themselves in the present moment and cultivate a sense of calm and tranquility. Through gentle observation of the breath, we can cultivate a deep awareness of our inner state and develop the ability to respond to life's challenges with clarity and equanimity.

Find a quiet and comfortable place to sit or lie down. Close your eyes if comfortable, or keep them gently focused on a spot in front of you.

Bring your attention to the natural rhythm of your breath. Notice the sensation of the breath as it enters and leaves your body.

Without trying to control your breath, simply observe its flow. Notice the rise and fall of your chest or the sensation of air passing through your nostrils.

If your mind starts to wander, gently guide your attention back to the breath. You can use a mental anchor, such as silently repeating "inhale" and "exhale" with each breath.

Continue to focus on the breath for a few minutes, gradually extending the duration of your meditation as you feel comfortable.

Body Scan Meditation

Body scan meditation is a practice that involves systematically scanning through different parts of the body, paying attention to sensations and feelings without judgment. This practice helps to develop a deep connection with the body and promotes relaxation and release of tension. By bringing mindful awareness to bodily sensations, practitioners can cultivate a greater sense of embodied presence and foster a harmonious relationship between mind and body.

Begin by finding a comfortable lying position, either on a yoga mat or your bed, with your arms by your sides and your legs uncrossed.

Close your eyes and take a few deep breaths to relax your body and mind.

Start by bringing your awareness to the top of your head. Notice any sensations, tension or areas of discomfort.

Slowly scan down through your body, paying attention to each part individually. Notice sensations in your face, neck, shoulders, arms, chest, abdomen, pelvis, legs, and feet.

As you scan through each body part, gently release any tension or discomfort you may notice. Imagine each breath flowing into that area, releasing any tightness or holding.

Continue scanning down your body until you reach your feet. Take a few moments to observe your body as a whole, noticing any changes in sensation or relaxation.

Walking Meditation

Walking meditation is a mindfulness practice that involves walking slowly and deliberately, paying attention to each step and the sensations associated with walking. This practice can be done indoors or outdoors and offers an opportunity to connect with the natural environment while cultivating mindfulness and presence. Walking meditation can be particularly beneficial for those who find it challenging to sit still for extended periods and prefer a more active approach to meditation.

Find a quiet and safe space where you can walk slowly and without distractions. It could be indoors or outdoors, such as a park or garden.

Begin by standing still and taking a few deep breaths to centre yourself. Feel the connection between your feet and the ground beneath you.

Start walking slowly, paying attention to each step you take. Notice the sensations in your feet as they lift, move forward, and touch the ground again.

As you walk, maintain a relaxed and natural pace. You can synchronise your steps with your breath, inhaling as you lift your foot and exhaling as you place it back down.

Notice the sights, sounds, and sensations around you as you walk. Stay present in the moment, letting go of any thoughts or distractions that arise.

Continue walking for a few minutes or as long as you like, allowing yourself to fully experience the practice of walking meditation.

Loving-Kindness Meditation

Loving-kindness meditation, also known as metta meditation, is a practice that involves cultivating feelings of love, compassion, and kindness towards oneself and others. This practice involves silently repeating phrases of well-wishes and extending feelings of love and compassion towards oneself, loved ones, acquaintances, and even challenging individuals. Loving-kindness meditation helps to cultivate a sense of connection and empathy, fostering inner harmony and emotional resilience.

Find a comfortable seated position and close your eyes. Take a few deep breaths to relax your body and mind

Begin by directing loving-kindness towards yourself. Silently repeat phrases such as "May I be happy, may I be healthy, may I be safe, may I live with ease.

Visualise yourself surrounded by feelings of love, compassion, and kindness. Imagine these qualities flowing into your heart and filling your entire being.

Next, extend loving-kindness towards a loved one. Visualise them in your mind's eye and silently repeat phrases such as "May you be happy, may you be healthy, may you be safe, may you live with ease.

Continue to extend loving-kindness towards other individuals, such as acquaintances, neutral people, and even challenging individuals. Repeat the phrases for each person, cultivating feelings of love and compassion

Finally, expand your loving-kindness to include all beings, everywhere. Visualise the entire world bathed in love and compassion, and silently repeat the phrases for the collective wellbeing of all.

Open Awareness Meditation

Open awareness meditation is a practice that involves resting in a state of open, non-directed awareness, allowing thoughts, feelings, and sensations to arise and pass without attachment or aversion. This practice helps to cultivate a spacious and receptive mind, free from the constraints of habitual thinking and reactive patterns. Open awareness meditation encourages a deep sense of acceptance and equanimity, fostering inner peace and harmony.

Begin by finding a comfortable seated position. You can sit on a cushion or a chair, ensuring that your spine is upright but relaxed. You can also lie down if that's more comfortable for you.
Take a few moments to set your intention for the practice. Open awareness meditation is about being present with whatever arises without judgment or attachment. You might set an intention to cultivate mindfulness, curiosity, or acceptance.

Start by bringing your attention to your breath. Notice the sensation of the breath as it enters and leaves your body. You can focus on the rising and falling of your chest or the feeling of air passing through your nostrils.

Once you feel settled, begin to expand your awareness to include all sensations, thoughts, and emotions present in your experience. Notice sounds in your environment, sensations in your body, and thoughts passing through your mind.

As you practice open awareness, allow everything to arise without judgment or attachment. Notice any tendencies to label experiences as "good" or "bad" and gently bring your attention back to the present.

Your mind may wander during the practice, and that's okay. When you notice your mind wandering, gently bring your attention back to your breath and the present moment. Each moment is an opportunity to begin again.

Approach your experience with curiosity and openness. Notice the ever-changing nature of your thoughts, sensations, and emotions. Allow yourself to explore each moment with a sense of wonder and interest.

As you continue to practice open awareness meditation, practice letting go of attachment to any particular experience. Allow each moment to unfold naturally, without trying to change or control anything.

After a period of open awareness meditation, take a few moments to reflect on your experience with gratitude. Notice any insights or shifts in awareness that may have arisen during the practice.

When you're ready, gently bring the meditation to a close. Take a few deep breaths, wiggle your fingers and toes, and slowly open your eyes. Carry the sense of openness and presence you cultivated during the practice into your daily life.

Meditation Techniques for Connecting with Inner Strength

Meditation is a profound practice for connecting with your inner strength and resilience. By cultivating a deep sense of awareness and presence, you can tap into the wellspring of strength and courage that resides within you. Here are some meditation techniques to help you access and harness your inner strength.

Grounding Meditation

This technique involves connecting with the present moment by focusing on the sensations of contact between your body and the ground beneath you. It helps promote feelings of stability, security, and presence.

Find a comfortable seated position or lie down with your palms facing upwards.

Close your eyes and take a few deep breaths to centre yourself. Visualise roots extending from the soles of your feet deep into the earth, anchoring you firmly to the ground.

Feel the stability and support of the earth beneath you, allowing it to nourish and energise you.

With each inhale, imagine drawing up strength and vitality from the earth into your body. Feel the energy coursing through you, filling you with a sense of groundedness and stability.

Mantra Meditation

In this practice, you repeat a word, phrase, or sound (Mantra) silently or aloud to focus your mind and evoke a sense of calm and clarity. Mantra meditation can help quiet the mind, reduce stress, and enhance concentration.

Choose a powerful mantra or affirmation that resonates with your inner strength. It could be a simple phrase like "I am strong," "I am resilient," or "I have the courage to overcome any challenge."

Sit comfortably in a quiet space and close your eyes. Take a few deep breaths to centre yourself and focus your mind.

Repeat your chosen mantra silently or aloud with each breath, allowing it to penetrate deep into your consciousness. Feel the words resonating within you, strengthening your resolve and fortifying your spirit.

Visualisation Meditation

Visualisation involves mentally picturing specific images, scenes, or scenarios to promote relaxation, healing, or personal growth. By engaging the imagination, visualisation meditation can enhance positive emotions, reduce anxiety, and manifest desired outcomes.

Close your eyes and envision yourself surrounded by a sphere of golden light, representing your inner strength and power.

Visualise this light expanding with each inhale, filling your entire body with radiant energy and vitality.

Feel the warmth and power of this light infusing every cell and fibre.

As you exhale, imagine releasing any doubts, fears, or insecurities that may be holding you back. Allow them to dissolve into the light, leaving you feeling lighter, clearer, and more empowered.

Breath Awareness Meditation

This technique involves focusing your attention on the breath, observing its rhythm, depth, and sensations without trying to control it. Breath awareness meditation promotes relaxation, mindfulness, and present-moment awareness, helping to calm the mind and reduce stress.

Sit comfortably with your spine straight and your hands resting on your knees. Close your eyes and bring your awareness to your breath.

Notice the sensation of the breath as it enters and leaves your body. Focus on the rise and fall of your chest or the feeling of air passing through your nostrils.

With each inhale, imagine drawing in strength and vitality. Feel your lungs expanding with fresh energy, revitalising every part of your body.

As you exhale, release any tension or negativity, letting go of anything that no longer serves you. Feel yourself becoming lighter and more buoyant with each breath.

Body Scan Meditation

In this practice, you systematically scan your body from head to toe, bringing awareness to each part and noticing any sensations, tension, or discomfort without judgment. Body scan meditation promotes relaxation, body awareness, and stress relief by encouraging physical and mental relaxation.

Lie down in a comfortable position and close your eyes. Take a few deep breaths to relax your body and calm your mind.

Begin by bringing your awareness to your feet. Notice any sensations you may be feeling, whether it's warmth, tingling, or pressure.

Slowly move your awareness up through your body, scanning each part from your feet to the top of your head. Notice any areas of tension or discomfort and consciously relax them with each exhale.

As you scan your body, cultivate a sense of inner strength and resilience. Visualise this strength radiating from within, infusing every cell and fibre of your being with courage and fortitude.

Practice these meditation techniques regularly to connect with your inner strength and cultivate a deep sense of resilience and empowerment. As you tap into your inner resources, you'll discover that you have the courage and strength to overcome any challenge that comes your way.

CHAPTER 9

SELF-CARE AND CHI RITUALS

Self-care is not just a luxury; it's essential for maintaining balance and resilience. It's about carving out time to recharge, replenish, and reconnect with ourselves on a deeper level. Chi plays a significant role in enhancing our self-care practices. When our Chi is balanced and flowing freely, we experience a sense of vitality and wellbeing.

Chi-Infused Beauty and Skincare Rituals

Incorporating Chi rituals into our self-care routine empowers us to honour our needs and prioritise our wellbeing. It's about creating sacred moments of self-reflection, mindfulness, and rejuvenation amid the hustle and bustle of daily life. Whether it's through gentle movement, breathwork, or mindful meditation, Chi rituals offer us a pathway to replenish our energy, reduce stress, and cultivate a sense of inner balance and harmony.

By embracing the wisdom of Chi and integrating it into our self-care practices, we can unlock our full potential for health, vitality, and holistic well-being. It's a journey of self-discovery and self-care that honours the innate wisdom of our bodies and nurtures the sacred connection between mind, body, and spirit.

Elevating Self-Care with Chi-Infused Beauty and Skincare Rituals

Let's dive into the transformative power of Chi-infused beauty and skincare rituals, exploring how these practices can elevate self-care routines to promote inner harmony, radiant skin, and a profound sense of wellbeing. Rooted in the ancient wisdom of Chi energy and modern skincare principles, these rituals offer a holistic approach to nurturing the body, mind, and spirit, embracing the interconnectedness of inner and outer beauty.

Chi-Infused Facial Massage

Chi-infused facial massage is a deeply relaxing and rejuvenating practice that combines the therapeutic benefits of touch with the nourishing properties of Chi-infused facial oils. This ritual not only promotes circulation and lymphatic drainage but also helps release tension held in the facial muscles, resulting in a glowing complexion and a sense of inner calm.

Chi-Infused Aromatherapy Facial Steam

A Chi-infused Aromatherapy facial steam is a luxurious self-care ritual that combines the therapeutic benefits of steam with the aromatic properties of Essential Oils. This ritual helps to open up the pores, cleanse the skin, and promote relaxation, leaving you with a radiant complexion and a sense of inner harmony.

Add a few drops of your favourite Chi-infused Essential Oil to a bowl of hot water. Choose an Essential Oil blend that resonates with your needs and preferences, such as lavender for relaxation, eucalyptus for respiratory support, or citrus for an uplifting boost.

Once you've added the Essential Oils, create a steam tent by draping a towel over your head and shoulders, positioning your face a comfortable distance from the bowl of hot water. Close your eyes and take slow, deep breaths, allowing the aromatic steam to envelop your senses and penetrate your pores.

Set a timer on your phone and relax and breathe deeply for 5-10 minutes, allowing the Chi-infused steam to work its magic on your skin and your mind. As you inhale the aromatic vapours, visualise yourself releasing tension and stress with each exhale, and feel your body and spirit becoming more balanced and harmonised.

After the facial steam, gently pat your skin dry with a clean towel and follow up with your favourite moisturiser or facial oil to lock in hydration and nourishment. Take a moment to admire your glowing complexion in the mirror, and bask in the rejuvenating effects of this Chi-infused self-care ritual.

Chi-Infused Aromatherapy Body Scrub

A Chi-infused Aromatherapy body scrub is a luxurious yet simple self-care ritual that combines the exfoliating benefits of a scrub with the aromatic properties of Essential Oils. This ritual helps to slough away dead skin cells, stimulate circulation, and promote a sense of renewal and vitality.

To create your own Chi-infused Aromatherapy body scrub, start by gathering your ingredients. You'll need a base scrub ingredient such as sugar or salt, a carrier oil such as coconut oil or almond oil, and your choice of Chi-infused Essential Oils.

In a small bowl, combine the base scrub ingredient with enough carrier oil to create a thick paste-like consistency. Add a few drops of your chosen Chi-infused Essential Oils to the mixture and stir well to combine. Choose Essential Oils that resonate with your intentions for the ritual, such as uplifting citrus oils for energy and vitality, grounding woody oils for stability and balance, or floral oils for beauty and grace.

Once you've mixed your Aromatherapy body scrub, step into the shower and wet your skin. Take a handful of the scrub mixture and gently massage it onto your skin using circular motions, focusing on areas that tend to be dry or rough such as elbows, knees, and heels.

As you massage the scrub into your skin, take a moment to connect with your breath and visualise yourself releasing any tension or negativity with each exhalation. Allow the aromatic scents of the Essential Oils to envelop your senses and uplift your mood, creating a sense of inner harmony and wellbeing.

After exfoliating your entire body, rinse off the scrub with warm water and pat your skin dry with a towel. Finally, moisturise with your favourite product. I promise you'll feel amazing.

Aromatherapy for Chi Balance

Aromatherapy, the practice of using aromatic Essential Oils to promote physical, emotional, and spiritual wellbeing, has been used for centuries to balance and harmonise the flow of Chi. Each Essential Oil carries its own unique energetic properties that can help to restore balance and vitality to the body, mind, and spirit.

Incorporating Chi-balancing and mood-enhancing Essential Oils into your daily Aromatherapy practice can help to harmonise and balance your energy flow, promote emotional wellbeing, and enhance your overall sense of vitality and vitality.

Facial Massage Techniques for Chi Activation

Facial massage is not only a luxurious self-care practice but also an effective way to activate Chi and promote balance and harmony throughout the body. By stimulating specific Acupressure points and energy channels on the face, you can enhance the flow of Chi, release tension, and rejuvenate your skin. Here are some simple yet effective facial massage techniques to help activate Chi.

My Tip: HotChi's Mindcare line has a range of facial oils blended with Aromatherapy oils and packaged in neat little dropper bottles. I carry at least one of their range around in my purse every day. They're great for a midday pick-me-up if you're flagging at your desk or just feel like a confidence boost. If you're wearing make up, you can massage into your décolleté (neck and chest), hands, even behind your knees for an instant healthy lift.

The duration of a facial massage session can vary depending on personal preference and available time. However, as a general guideline, a facial massage session typically lasts around 2 to 10 minutes. This duration allows enough time to effectively massage the key areas of the face while still being manageable to incorporate into a daily self-care routine.

It's essential to listen to your body and adjust the duration based on your individual needs and preferences. Some days, you may prefer a shorter massage session to quickly refresh and rejuvenate your skin, while other days, you may opt for a longer pamper session to indulge in a more thorough and relaxing experience.

Ultimately, the goal of facial massage is to promote relaxation, improve circulation, and enhance overall wellbeing. Therefore, whether you choose to massage for 2 minutes or 10 minutes, the most important aspect is to enjoy the experience and reap the benefits of this self-care practice. Here are some simple yet effective facial massage techniques to help release your Chi:

Forehead Massage

Benefits: Massaging the forehead helps release tension in the frontal muscles and temples, promoting relaxation and reducing headaches. Stimulating the Acupressure points in this area can also help relieve stress and improve mental clarity, contributing to a sense of balance and harmony.

Technique: Start by placing your fingertips at the centre of your forehead, between your eyebrows. Gently massage in circular motions, moving outward towards your temples. Repeat this motion several times to release tension and promote relaxation.

Eyebrow Massage

Benefits: Massaging the eyebrows stimulates blood circulation in the area, which can help reduce puffiness and dark circles. It also promotes relaxation of the eye muscles and alleviates tension, contributing to improved eye health and overall wellbeing.

Technique: Use your index and middle fingers to massage along your eyebrows, starting from the inner corners and moving outward towards your temples. Apply gentle pressure to stimulate the Acupressure points along the eyebrows and promote circulation in the area.

Cheek Massage

Benefits: Massaging the cheeks stimulates the facial muscles and promotes lymphatic drainage, reducing puffiness and promoting a more sculpted appearance. It also enhances circulation, delivering oxygen and nutrients to the skin cells, resulting in a radiant complexion and improved skin health.

Technique: With your fingertips, massage your cheeks in upward circular motions, starting from the corners of your mouth and moving towards your ears. Apply gentle pressure to stimulate the Acupressure points on your cheeks and promote lymphatic drainage.

Jawline Massage

Benefits: Massaging the jawline helps release tension in the jaw muscles and temporomandibular joint (TMJ), reducing jaw pain and discomfort. It also stimulates the lymphatic system, promoting detoxification and reducing fluid retention in the face, resulting in a more defined jawline and improved facial contour.

Technique: Use your thumbs to massage along your jawline, starting from the centre of your chin and moving towards your ears. Apply firm pressure to release tension in the jaw muscles and promote relaxation.

Temple Massage

Benefits: Massaging the temples helps relieve tension and reduce headaches by stimulating blood circulation and promoting relaxation. It also calms the mind and soothes stress-related symptoms, contributing to overall wellbeing and mental clarity.

Technique: With your fingertips, massage your temples in circular motions, moving in a clockwise direction. Apply gentle pressure to release tension and promote relaxation.

Nasolabial Fold Massage

Benefits: Massaging the nasolabial folds, the lines that run from the sides of your nose to the corners of your mouth, helps smooth out fine lines and wrinkles in the area, promoting a more youthful appearance. It also stimulates circulation and lymphatic drainage, reducing puffiness and promoting collagen production, resulting in firmer, plumper skin.

Technique: Gently massage the nasolabial folds using upward circular motions. This helps to stimulate circulation in the area and reduce the appearance of fine lines and wrinkles.

Under-Eye Massage

Benefits: Massaging the under-eye area helps reduce puffiness and dark circles by promoting lymphatic drainage and increasing blood circulation. It also stimulates collagen production, reducing the appearance of fine lines and wrinkles, and promoting a brighter, more refreshed look.

Technique: Use your ring fingers to gently massage the area under your eyes in outward circular motions. Be careful not to apply too much pressure, as the skin in this area is delicate. This massage helps to reduce puffiness and dark circles and promote lymphatic drainage.

Ear Massage

Benefits: Massaging the ears stimulates the Acupressure points located on the ears, which are connected to various organs and systems in the body. This promotes Chi flow throughout the body, balancing energy levels and enhancing overall health and vitality.

Technique: Gently massage your earlobes and the outer edges of your ears using your thumb and index finger. Pay special attention to the Acupressure points located on the ears, as massaging these points can help to stimulate Chi flow throughout the body.

Scalp Massage

Benefits: Massaging the scalp helps relax the scalp muscles and improve blood circulation to the hair follicles, promoting hair growth and overall scalp health. It also stimulates the release of endorphins, reducing stress and promoting relaxation, contributing to a sense of wellbeing.

Technique: Finish your facial massage routine with a relaxing scalp massage. Don't be afraid to use diluted Essential Oils on your scalp. Use your fingertips to massage your scalp in circular motions, starting from the front and moving towards the back of your head. This helps to release tension in the scalp muscles and promote relaxation.

By incorporating these facial massage techniques into your daily self-care routine, you can experience a wide range of benefits, including improved skin health, reduced tension and stress, and enhanced overall wellbeing. Plus you'll smell great!

Creating Personalised Chi Rituals for Self-Care

Let's explore how to create personalised Chi rituals for self-care, tailored to your unique needs and preferences. As you become more familiar with what works best for you, you'll notice significant improvements in your inner beauty,

Identify Your Intentions

Begin by identifying your intentions and goals for your Chi rituals. What aspects of your physical, emotional, and spiritual wellbeing would you like to focus on? Whether it's reducing stress, promoting relaxation, boosting energy, or enhancing mindfulness, clarifying your intentions will guide the design of your personalised rituals.

Choose Ritual Components

Select the components you'd like to include in your Chi rituals based on your intentions. This could include practices such as breathwork with Aromatherapy, meditation, Acupressure, yoga or any other techniques that resonate with you. Consider incorporating elements from different modalities to create a holistic and balanced approach to self-care.

Create a Ritual Space

Designate a quiet and comfortable space where you can practice your Chi rituals without distractions. Set the ambiance by incorporating elements such as soft lighting, calming music and aromatic Essential Oils to create a serene and inviting atmosphere conducive to relaxation and introspection.

Set Your Intention

Before beginning your ritual, take a moment to set your intention and focus your mind on your desired outcome. This could be done through a simple meditation or visualisation exercise where you envision yourself embodying the qualities you wish to cultivate during the ritual.

Follow a Ritual Sequence
Develop a structured sequence for your self-care Chi rituals that incorporates the chosen components in a systematic manner. For example, you might start with a grounding breathwork exercise to centre yourself, followed by a guided meditation to promote relaxation, and conclude with an Aromatherapy self-massage to soothe your senses.

Practice Consistently
Consistency is key to reaping the benefits of your Chi rituals. Make a commitment to practice your personalised rituals regularly, whether it's daily, weekly, or as often as your schedule allows. Set aside dedicated time for your rituals and prioritise self-care as an essential part of your overall beauty routine.

Reflect and Adjust
After each ritual, take a moment to reflect on your experience and observe how you feel physically, emotionally, and mentally. Notice any changes or shifts in your energy levels, mood, or overall wellbeing. Based on your observations, make any necessary adjustments to your ritual components or sequence to better align with your needs and preferences.

Stay Open to Adaptation
As you continue to explore and refine your Chi rituals, remain open to adaptation and experimentation. Allow your practice to evolve organically over time, incorporating new techniques or modifying existing ones as you deepen your understanding of yourself and your needs.

By creating personalised Chi rituals for self-care, you can cultivate a deeper connection with your inner wisdom, promote holistic wellbeing, and nurture a sense of balance and harmony in your life.

CHAPTER 10

EMPOWERING CONFIDENCE WITH CHI

Young women face a myriad of challenges that can take a toll on their confidence, self-esteem, and overall wellbeing. From the lingering effects of isolation caused by the Covid-19 pandemic to the everyday pressures of navigating relationships, career aspirations, and societal expectations, the journey to self-confidence and empowerment can often feel like an uphill battle.

The Covid-19 pandemic and its associated restrictions have significantly impacted the lives of young women around the world. For many, the sudden transition to remote work or virtual learning, coupled with social distancing measures, led to feelings of isolation, loneliness, and disconnection from their support networks. As the world gradually reopened, many young women were left grappling with the aftermath of this prolonged period of isolation, trying to rebuild social connections and adjust to a new normal.

Furthermore, the pressures of modern society, fuelled by social media and unrealistic beauty standards, can exacerbate feelings of self-doubt and inadequacy among young women. The constant comparison to curated online personas and the pressure to portray a flawless image can erode self-confidence and contribute to negative self-talk.

In my professional career as a psychologist specialising in the unique issues facing teenage girls and young women, I saw a 10x increase in face-to-face appointments after the pandemic and over

100x increase in virtual sessions. If proof were needed that we need help to navigate this often brutal and unforgiving world we live in, I probably helped more young women in the past four years than in my previous 30 year career!

In the face of these challenges, it's essential for young women to cultivate resilience, self-compassion, and inner strength to navigate life's ups and downs with confidence and grace. This chapter explores how Chi practices can empower young women to build confidence, overcome self-doubt, and embrace their true selves authentically. Through a combination of mindfulness techniques, positive affirmations, and self-care rituals, young women can harness the power of Chi to cultivate a deep sense of self-worth and resilience in the face of adversity. Let's dive into the transformative journey of empowering confidence with Chi.

Building Confidence through Chi Practices

Confidence is not an innate trait but rather a skill that can be developed and nurtured over time. For young women navigating the complexities of modern life, cultivating confidence is essential for asserting themselves in various spheres, from the workplace to personal relationships. Chi practices offer a holistic approach to building confidence by addressing the mind, body, and spirit. In this sub-section, we explore how Chi practices can empower young women to cultivate unwavering confidence from within.

Harnessing the Power of Breath: Conscious Breathing for Confidence

The breath is a powerful tool for grounding and centring oneself, especially in moments of doubt or anxiety. Conscious breathing techniques, such as diaphragmatic breathing and square breathing, can help young women regulate their emotions and access a state of calm confidence. By practicing mindful breathing exercises regularly, young women can train their bodies to respond to stress with resilience and poise, laying the foundation for lasting confidence.

Embracing Mindfulness Meditation: Cultivating Inner Strength and Self-Awareness

Mindfulness meditation is a practice of cultivating present-moment awareness and non-judgmental acceptance of one's thoughts and emotions. By incorporating mindfulness meditation into their daily routine, young women can develop a deeper understanding of their inner landscape and cultivate self-awareness. This heightened self-awareness allows them to identify and challenge limiting beliefs and negative self-talk, paving the way for increased confidence and self-assurance.

Affirmations and Positive Self-Talk: Rewiring the Mind for Confidence

Affirmations are powerful tools for reprogramming the subconscious mind and fostering a positive self-image. Young women can harness the power of affirmations by incorporating positive statements into their daily routine, such as "I am confident and capable" or "I trust in my abilities to overcome challenges." By consistently reinforcing positive self-talk, young women can cultivate a resilient mindset and bolster their confidence in their abilities to navigate life's challenges.

Self-Care Rituals: Nurturing the Body and Mind for Confidence

Self-care is an essential component of building confidence, as it allows young women to prioritise their wellbeing and recharge their mental and emotional batteries. Incorporating self-care rituals, such as skincare routines, yoga practice, or journaling, into their daily lives can help young women cultivate a sense of self-worth and confidence. These rituals serve as acts of self-love and validation, reinforcing the belief that they are deserving of care and respect.

By integrating these Chi practices into their daily lives, young women can build a strong foundation of confidence that emanates from within. With mindful breathing, mindfulness meditation, positive affirmations, and self-care rituals, young women can cultivate unwavering confidence and resilience, enabling them to navigate life's challenges with grace and poise.

Chi Techniques for Overcoming Self-Doubt

Self-doubt is a common obstacle that many young women face on their journey toward confidence and self-assurance. Whether stemming from societal pressures, past experiences, or internalised beliefs, self-doubt can undermine one's sense of worth and hinder personal growth. In this sub-section, we explore various Chi techniques that young women can employ to overcome self-doubt and cultivate a mindset of empowerment.

Visualisation and Manifestation: Harnessing the Power of the Mind

Visualisation is a powerful technique for reprogramming the subconscious mind and overcoming self-doubt. By vividly imagining themselves achieving their goals and embodying confidence, young women can create a mental blueprint for success. Combined with manifestation practices, such as creating vision boards or journaling, visualisation can help young women align their thoughts and actions with their desired outcomes, fostering a sense of self-belief and empowerment.

Energy Clearing and Rebalancing: Releasing Limiting Beliefs

Self-doubt often stems from internalised beliefs and negative thought patterns that create energetic blocks within the body. Energy clearing techniques, such as breathwork, meditation, and Reiki, can help young women identify and release these limiting beliefs, allowing for greater emotional and energetic freedom. By regularly clearing and rebalancing their energy field, young women can create space for self-confidence to flourish and thrive.

Affirmative Action: Taking Bold Steps Toward Growth

Action is a powerful antidote to self-doubt, as it provides tangible evidence of one's capabilities and potential for growth. By setting small, achievable goals and taking affirmative action steps toward them, young women can build momentum and confidence in their abilities. Whether it's signing up for a class, volunteering for a project, or speaking up in a meeting, each action taken serves as a testament to their courage and resilience, gradually eroding self-doubt and reinforcing self-belief.

Self-Compassion and Forgiveness: Cultivating Inner Resilience

Self-compassion is an essential practice for overcoming self-doubt and cultivating inner resilience. By practicing self-compassion, young women can learn to treat themselves with kindness and understanding, especially in moments of failure or setback. Additionally, forgiveness practices, both for oneself and others, can help release the grip of past mistakes and free up mental and emotional energy for growth and self-discovery. By cultivating self-compassion and forgiveness, young women can foster a sense of inner peace and acceptance, allowing for greater self-confidence to emerge.

Through the consistent application of these Chi techniques, young women can overcome self-doubt and cultivate a mindset of empowerment and self-assurance. By harnessing the power of visualisation, energy clearing, affirmative action, and self-compassion, young women can break free from the shackles of self-doubt and step into their full potential with confidence and resilience.

Cultivating Self-Compassion and Positive Self-Talk with Chi

Self-compassion and positive self-talk are essential components of building confidence and resilience in young women. In this sub-section, we explore how Chi practices can be utilised to cultivate self-compassion and promote positive self-talk, leading to greater emotional wellbeing and self-assurance.

Mindfulness Meditation: Cultivating Present-Moment Awareness

Mindfulness meditation is a powerful tool for cultivating self-compassion and positive self-talk by fostering present-moment awareness and acceptance of one's thoughts and emotions. Through regular mindfulness practice, young women can develop a non-judgmental attitude toward themselves and cultivate a sense of self-compassion that is rooted in kindness and understanding. By observing their thoughts with curiosity and compassion, rather than judgment or criticism, young women can reframe negative self-talk and cultivate a more positive and empowering inner dialogue.

Loving-Kindness Meditation: Cultivating Compassion Toward Oneself and Others

Loving-kindness meditation, also known as Metta meditation, is a practice focused on cultivating feelings of love, compassion, and kindness toward oneself and others. By engaging in loving-kindness meditation regularly, young women can develop a sense of self-compassion that extends beyond themselves to encompass all beings. Through the repetition of loving-kindness phrases, such as "May I be happy, may I be healthy, may I be safe, may I be at ease," young women can cultivate a sense of inner warmth and self-care that counteracts negative self-talk and fosters greater emotional resilience.

Affirmations and Mantras: Rewriting the Inner Narrative

Affirmations and mantras are powerful tools for rewiring the brain and promoting positive self-talk. By intentionally choosing and repeating affirming statements or mantras, young women can counteract negative self-talk and cultivate a more empowering inner narrative. Whether reciting affirmations related to self-worth, resilience, or personal strengths, or chanting uplifting mantras derived from ancient wisdom traditions, young women can harness the power of positive language to shift their mindset and cultivate greater self-compassion and confidence.

Journaling and Self-Reflection: Uncovering Inner Truths and Insights

Journaling and self-reflection are valuable practices for cultivating self-compassion and positive self-talk by providing a space for young women to explore their thoughts, feelings, and experiences in a non-judgmental and compassionate way. Through journaling prompts focused on self-compassion, gratitude, and personal growth, young women can uncover inner truths and insights that promote greater self-awareness and self-acceptance. By regularly engaging in journaling and self-reflection, young women can cultivate a deeper sense of self-compassion and develop a more positive and empowering inner dialogue.

Through the consistent practice of mindfulness meditation, loving-kindness meditation, affirmations and mantras, and journaling and self-reflection, young women can cultivate self-compassion and positive self-talk, leading to greater emotional wellbeing, resilience, and confidence in themselves and their abilities. By nurturing a kind and supportive inner dialogue, young women can navigate life's challenges with greater ease and grace, knowing that they are worthy of love, kindness, and compassion

Using Chi to Enhance Assertiveness and Presence

Assertiveness and presence are essential qualities that can greatly influence success and fulfilment in various aspects of life, including personal relationships, career advancement, and self-development.

Assertiveness is the ability to express one's thoughts, feelings, and needs openly and confidently while respecting the rights and boundaries of others. It involves communicating assertively without being passive or aggressive, asserting oneself appropriately in different situations, and standing up for one's beliefs and values. When individuals are in tune with their Chi, they often experience a sense of inner strength, self-assurance, and clarity of purpose, which are essential components of assertiveness.

Presence, on the other hand, refers to the ability to be fully engaged and present in the moment, both physically and mentally. It involves being mindful, attentive, and focused on the task at hand, whether it's a social interaction, a professional meeting, or a personal endeavour. Cultivating presence requires individuals to connect with their inner selves, tap into their intuition, and project authenticity and confidence outwardly. When individuals align with their Chi, they often radiate a strong and commanding presence that draws others to them and commands respect.

In conclusion, this chapter has looked into the empowering realm of confidence with Chi. We explored various Chi practices and techniques aimed at building confidence, overcoming self-doubt, cultivating self-compassion, and enhancing assertiveness among young women. Through the integration of Chi into daily rituals and practices, young women can harness the power of Chi to boost their self-esteem, develop a positive mindset, and navigate life's challenges with resilience and grace.

By setting intentions, designing personalised rituals, tailoring practices to individual needs, and cultivating consistency in their Chi practices, you can foster a deeper connection with your inner strength and resilience. As you embark on your journey of self-discovery and personal growth, Chi becomes a guiding force that empowers you to embrace your unique potential, overcome obstacles, and thrive in all aspects of your life.

CHAPTER 11

THE SCIENCE OF SEXUAL WELLNESS

Let's now explore the foundational science of sexual wellness, including how you can build confidence and connection with Chi-related practices and mindfulness techniques that can help you overcome insecurities, harness the power of self-affirmation, and embrace body positivity. By incorporating these practices into a conscious routine, you can cultivate the confidence needed to fully explore and enjoy your sexuality without inhibition or fear, resulting in a deeper connection to both yourself and your partner.

We'll begin by understanding how Chi practices can empower us and our partner to embrace our unique beauty and sexuality. Through mindfulness exercises and self-reflection, we'll learn to identify and challenge limiting beliefs that may be holding us back from fully embracing our sexuality.

We'll explore the transformative power of self-affirmation and mindful practices in building confidence from within. By cultivating a positive and empowering inner dialogue, we'll develop greater self-assurance and resilience in navigating sexual experiences and relationships.

And we'll discuss practical techniques for embracing body positivity and nurturing a positive relationship with our body and sexuality. Through Chi-inspired self-care rituals and self-love practices, you'll learn to celebrate your body's beauty and embrace your sexuality with confidence and grace.

Confidence and Self-Affirmation

Confidence is the cornerstone of sexual wellbeing, governing how we perceive ourselves, interact with our partners, and experience pleasure. Here we explore how Chi practices can help you overcome insecurities, cultivate self-assurance, and harness the power of self-affirmation to unlock your sexual potential.

Overcoming Insecurities with Chi Practices

Research consistently shows that both women and men struggle with insecurities related to body image, performance anxiety, and self-worth, which can significantly impact their sexual confidence. However, Chi practices offer a holistic approach to overcoming these insecurities and embracing one's sexuality with confidence. By incorporating mindfulness techniques, such as meditation and visualisation, we can develop greater self-awareness and self-acceptance, allowing us to let go of limiting beliefs and negative self-talk. Additionally, practices like Acupressure and Chi breathing can help release tension and promote relaxation, allowing us to feel more comfortable and present in our bodies during sexual experiences.

Cultivating Confidence through Mindful Practices

Mindfulness practices have been shown to be highly effective in boosting confidence and self-esteem. By practicing mindfulness, we can learn to observe our thoughts and emotions without judgment, allowing us to cultivate a more positive and empowering mindset. Techniques such as body scanning and progressive muscle relaxation can help all women develop a deeper connection with their bodies and foster a sense of inner strength and resilience. Moreover, mindfulness practices can enhance self-awareness and emotional regulation, empowering women to navigate sexual situations with confidence and ease.

Harnessing the Power of Self-Affirmation

Self-affirmation is a powerful tool for boosting confidence and self-esteem. Research has shown that regularly engaging in self-affirmation exercises can lead to improvements in mood, self-perception, and overall wellbeing. Through Chi-inspired self-affirmation practices, women can cultivate a more positive and compassionate relationship with themselves, challenging negative self-perceptions and embracing their inherent worth and value. By affirming our strengths, values, and achievements, we can build a solid foundation of self-confidence that extends into all areas of our lives, including our sexual experiences.

Sensory Sensations and Aromatherapy

The sense of smell holds a unique and powerful sway over our emotions and memories. As the most primitive of our senses, smell has the remarkable ability to evoke vivid memories, stir deep emotions, and even elicit sexual arousal. This phenomenon is rooted in the intricate workings of the olfactory system, where odour molecules bind to receptors in the nasal cavity, triggering a cascade of neural signals that are processed in the brain's limbic system—the seat of emotion and memory.

Chi practices offer a transformative approach to harnessing the sensual potential of scent. By incorporating mindfulness techniques and intentional breathing exercises, we can amplify the impact of Aromatherapy on our sexual experience. Through focused attention and conscious awareness, Chi practices heighten sensitivity to scent, allowing us to immerse ourselves fully in the sensual pleasures of aroma.

Using Essential Oils to Enhance Arousal

Essential Oils, derived from aromatic plants and botanicals, are prized for their therapeutic properties and tantalising scents. These potent elixirs offer a natural and holistic approach to enhancing arousal and intimacy. When applied topically or diffused into the air, Essential Oils release volatile compounds that stimulate the olfactory receptors, triggering a cascade of physiological responses that promote relaxation, arousal, and heightened sensitivity.

Chi practices provide a framework for incorporating Essential Oils into sensual rituals and intimate encounters. By infusing facial oils, massage oils, bath blends, or room sprays with carefully selected Essential Oils, you can create an atmosphere of sensuality and romance that elevates the sexual experience. Through intentional touch and mindful presence, Chi practitioners can deepen their connection with themselves and their partners, fostering intimacy and pleasure.

Women who have higher scent sensitivity report more orgasms than women who do not. So if you have a good nose, your sexual wellbeing will benefit from using Essential Oils. Look out for products with these Essential Oils for aphrodisiac effects for women: Clary Sage, Lavender, Sandalwood and Ylang Ylang.

Creating Romantic Atmospheres with Scent

The ambiance of a space plays a pivotal role in setting the stage for intimacy and connection. Scent, in particular, has the power to transform an ordinary environment into a haven of sensuality and romance. Whether through the flicker of scented candles, the waft of aromatic diffusers, or the subtle infusion of natural fragrances, scent can evoke feelings of warmth, passion, and desire.

Chi practices offer a holistic approach to creating romantic atmospheres with scent. By infusing the environment with carefully curated aromas that resonate with your personal preferences and desires, you can cultivate an ambiance that fosters intimacy and arousal.

Inner Beauty and Self-Love

Confidence serves as a catalyst for self-expression, exploration, and pleasure. By nurturing inner confidence, we can cultivate a radiant sense of self-assurance that shines through in interactions and relationships. Chi practices offer a pathway to inner radiance, empowering us to embrace our unique qualities and celebrate our inherent worthiness.

Through mindfulness techniques, affirmations, and self-care rituals, Chi practitioners can foster a deep sense of confidence and self-assurance. By acknowledging and embracing their strengths, passions, and desires, individuals can cultivate a positive self-image that serves as a foundation for sexual empowerment and fulfilment. With each mindful breath and intentional gesture, individuals can tap into their inner reservoir of confidence, allowing their inner radiance to shine brightly. And as we've discussed earlier, confidence is contagious. Your positive actions can work wonders on your partner by creating deep connections.

Embracing Your Unique Beauty and Sexuality

True beauty emanates from within, radiating outward in a luminous display of authenticity and self-expression. Embrace your unique beauty and sexuality to unlock a profound sense of empowerment and liberation. Chi practices provide a framework for embracing your inherent beauty and celebrating the full spectrum of your sexuality.

Through mindfulness exercises, body-positive affirmations, and sensual self-care practices, you can cultivate a deep sense of appreciation for your body and your sexuality. By acknowledging and honouring your desires, preferences, and boundaries, you can embrace your unique beauty with confidence and grace. With each act of self-love and acceptance, you nurture a profound connection with yourself, fostering a sense of wholeness and fulfilment.

Enhancing Self-Love and Appreciation

Self-love is a transformative practice that encompasses acceptance, compassion, and forgiveness. By engaging in practices that nurture self-love and appreciation, you can cultivate a deep sense of connection and contentment within yourself. Chi practices offer a myriad of techniques for enhancing self-love and appreciation, ranging from mindfulness meditation to self-care rituals.

Through daily affirmations, gratitude practices, and acts of self-care, learn to foster a deep sense of self-appreciation. Acknowledge your worthiness and embrace your imperfections, to cultivate a profound sense of self-love that transcends external validation. With each loving gesture and compassionate thought, you can nourish your inner radiance, fostering a deep sense of wellbeing and fulfilment.

Relaxation Techniques and Sensual Bliss

In this section, we explore the profound connection between relaxation techniques and sensual bliss, exploring practices that promote deep relaxation, enhance tactile sensations, and elevate the overall sexual experience.

Techniques for Achieving Deep Relaxation
Deep relaxation forms the foundation of sensual bliss, creating an optimal state for experiencing pleasure and intimacy. Chi practices offer a variety of techniques for achieving a relaxed state, ranging from mindfulness meditation to progressive muscle relaxation. By quieting the mind and releasing tension from the body, we can create a spacious and receptive mindspace for sensual exploration and connection.

Through guided imagery, visualisation exercises, and body-scan techniques, we can cultivate a profound sense of calm and tranquility, allowing us to fully immerse ourselves in the present moment. With each mindful breath and gentle release of tension, we sink deeper into a state of relaxation, opening ourselves to the full spectrum of sensory experiences and pleasures.

Incorporating Massage and Touch for Relaxation
Massage and touch are powerful tools for promoting relaxation and enhancing sensual connection. Chi practices encourage the incorporation of massage and touch into intimate encounters, allowing individuals to deepen their bond and heighten their sensory experiences. By incorporating gentle touch, caresses, and massage techniques, partners can create a nurturing and pleasurable environment conducive to relaxation and sensual exploration.

Through mindful touch exercises, couples can explore the intricacies of tactile sensation, fostering a deeper connection and understanding of each other's bodies. By attuning to each other's needs and preferences, we can create a safe and supportive space for mutual relaxation and pleasure. With each loving touch and tender gesture, we can cultivate a profound sense of intimacy and bliss, deepening a connection that enhances sexual experiences.

Breathing Exercises to Enhance Relaxation and Sensuality

Breath is the bridge between the body and the mind, serving as a powerful tool for enhancing relaxation and sensuality. Chi practices emphasise the importance of conscious breathing in promoting relaxation and deepening the sexual experience. By engaging in breathwork exercises, individuals can regulate their nervous system, quiet their thoughts, and heighten their awareness of sensation.

Through rhythmic breathing, breath awareness, and pranayama techniques, individuals can synchronise their breath with their partner's, creating a harmonious and deeply connected experience. By focusing on the breath, we can anchor ourselves in the present moment, allowing us to fully experience the pleasure and intimacy of the moment. With each mindful inhale and exhale, we tap into a profound sense of relaxation and sensuality, enriching our sexual encounters and deepening our connection with our partner.

In conclusion, this chapter explored the transformative power of relaxation techniques and their profound impact on sensual bliss. Through practices such as deep relaxation, massage and touch, and breathwork, we can create a supportive and nurturing environment conducive to deepening our connection to ourselves and our partner, and enhancing our sexual experiences. By cultivating a state of relaxation and presence, we can tap into the full spectrum of sensory pleasures and experiences, fostering a sense of intimacy, connection, and fulfilment in our sexual encounters.

CHAPTER 12

INTEGRATING CHI INTO DAILY LIFE

Finding balance and harmony amidst the chaos of daily life can feel like an elusive goal. From navigating work demands to managing personal relationships and caring for our wellbeing, the constant juggling act can leave us feeling overwhelmed and disconnected from ourselves.

Understand the true power of Chi offers a profound perspective on how we can infuse every aspect of our lives with intention, mindfulness, and vitality. In this chapter, we will explore how to integrate Chi into our daily routines and activities, creating a harmonious and balanced way of living that promotes holistic wellbeing and inner peace.

By incorporating Chi principles into our everyday activities, creating Chi-inspired living spaces, practicing mindful eating and nutrition, and embracing Chi practices for enhancing sleep and rest, we can cultivate a deeper connection with ourselves, our surroundings, and the world around us. Through the practice of Chi in daily life, we can tap into our innate vitality, wisdom, and resilience, allowing us to live each day with greater mindfulness, presence, and joy.

Chi in Everyday Activities and Routines

Incorporating Chi principles into our daily activities and routines is essential for fostering a sense of balance, vitality, and mindfulness in our lives. Whether it's our morning rituals, work tasks, or evening wind-down, infusing Chi into our everyday activities can help us cultivate a deeper connection with ourselves and the world around us. Here, we'll explore various ways to integrate Chi into our daily lives:

Morning Chi Rituals

Start your day with a mindful Chi ritual to set a positive tone for the day ahead. Begin by taking a few moments to connect with your breath and centre yourself.

Practice gentle stretching or Chi-enhancing exercises to awaken your body and stimulate energy flow.

Engage in a Chi-infused morning meditation to cultivate inner peace and mental clarity.

Set intentions for the day, focusing on qualities like gratitude, compassion, and presence.

Chi in Work Tasks

Incorporate Chi principles into your work routine to enhance focus, productivity, and creativity. Take regular breaks to stretch, breathe deeply, and recalibrate your energy.

Practice mindful breathing while tackling challenging tasks to stay grounded and centred.

Create a Chi-friendly work environment by incorporating elements like natural light, plants, and calming scents.

Chi-infused Movement

Infuse everyday movements with Chi by focusing on intention, breath, and presence. Practice mindful walking, paying attention to each step and the sensations in your body.

Incorporate Chi-enhancing exercises like Qi Gong or Tai Chi into your daily routine to promote balance and vitality.

Take opportunities throughout the day to move your body mindfully, whether it's stretching at your desk, taking a walk outside, or practicing yoga.

Evening Chi Practices

Wind down your day with Chi-enhancing evening rituals to promote relaxation and restful sleep. Engage in gentle movement practices like restorative yoga or Chi-inspired stretches to release tension from the day.

Practice deep breathing exercises or meditation to quiet the mind and prepare for rest.

Create a soothing bedtime routine that includes activities like reading, journaling, or listening to calming music to promote relaxation.

Learn what works best for you and once your routines become second-nature to you, you will find yourself looking forward to these small but mighty exercises.

My Tip: I found out many years ago that sitting perfectly still and silent in class, at work or even on our daily commute, we become aware of everything around us. We become super-sensitive to other's emotions and natural vibes. Use this time to practice your breathwork and meditation. Apart from feeling in total control of ourselves, you'll give the outward impression of being calm, focused and strong. Remember, being the loudest in the room doesn't make you a leader but being the calmest does. Think of Steve Jobs, Rihanna and Barack Obama.

Creating Chi-Inspired Living Spaces

Our living and working spaces play a significant role in shaping our overall wellbeing and energy levels. By designing our environments with Chi principles in mind, we can create harmonious and nurturing spaces that support our physical, emotional, and spiritual wellbeing.

I had a patient recently that was very meticulous about the neatness of her desk space. She made sure it was clear and tidy at all times with her pens, papers, files and personal items arranged in a very particular way. She became anxious if a work colleague moved anything, or heaven forbid, borrowed an item. She explained to me that the "aesthetic" of her personal space was important to her, as she needed to feel everything had its place. I love this story because we successfully transitioned her from a negative feeling of anxious control to one of recognising that this simple quirk was her way of unblocking her natural flow of Chi. Rather than seeing her desk space as a protected area, she now sees it as a symbol of her uncluttered mind. This might sound like a tiny change, but as you've learned, little changes can make big differences. Here are some key ways to infuse Chi into our personal spaces.

Decluttering and Simplifying

Begin by decluttering your living or working space to create a sense of openness and flow. Clear out any unnecessary items that no longer serve you and organise your belongings in a way that promotes ease and accessibility. Simplify your décor and furnishings to create a calming and uncluttered environment. Opt for clean lines, natural materials, and neutral colours to create a sense of tranquility and balance.

With the rise of post-pandemic work from home options for many employees, it's important our workspace and our living space do not conflict with each other. Just as we need a clear emotional delineation between the end of the work day and the start of our social evening (hello Happy Hour), the same applies to a physical separation between work and play.

For some people—in particular young people that don't have the room for a separate home office—they often hang out at Starbucks all day with their laptop (this creates a whole other set of problems about social isolation I've covered elsewhere in this book, but the bottom line is don't spend all day in Starbucks on your own thinking you're getting lots done).

I advise many corporations on office layout and flow and I was asked to investigate why productivity had declined sharply at a Fortune 500 company that had recently allowed its employees to work from home. There could have been many reasons—people slacking off, being distracted by their cat (guilty!) or just not being in the "zone".

My first instinct proved right and those workers that didn't have a dedicated work-from-home area—or even a proper desk and office chair—were the most impacted with declining performance. The solution, as is often the case with human behaviour, was quite simple. I advised the company to send small desks, proper office chairs and general office supplies to their workers' homes to ensure they could create an effective working environment. Little changes, big differences.

Natural Elements

Incorporate natural elements into your living space to connect with the earth's energy and create a sense of grounding. Introduce plants, natural wood, stones, and other organic materials to bring a sense of vitality and harmony to your surroundings.

Maximise natural light in your space by opening curtains and blinds during the day and arranging furniture to allow light to flow freely. Natural light not only brightens your space but also uplifts your mood and energy levels.

Flow and Balance

Pay attention to the flow of energy in your living space by arranging furniture and décor in a way that promotes a smooth and uninterrupted flow. Avoid placing furniture in direct pathways or blocking doorways and windows.

Create balance and harmony in your space by incorporating elements of symmetry and proportion. Arrange furniture and décor in balanced groupings and use mirrors to reflect light and energy throughout the room.

Sacred Spaces and Altars

Designate a sacred space or altar in your home where you can connect with your inner self and cultivate a sense of reverence and gratitude. This could be a small corner of a room or a dedicated altar space where you can display meaningful objects, photos, or symbols that inspire you.

Personalise your sacred space with items that hold special significance to you, such as crystals, candles, incense, or spiritual artefacts. Use this space for daily rituals, meditation, or reflection to enhance your connection with the divine and cultivate inner peace.

By infusing our living spaces with Chi principles such as decluttering, incorporating natural elements, promoting flow and balance, and creating sacred spaces, we can cultivate environments that support our overall wellbeing and enhance our connection with ourselves and the world around us. These simple yet powerful practices can transform our living and work spaces into sanctuaries of peace, harmony, and vitality, nurturing our body, mind, and spirit.

Mindful Eating and Nutrition for Chi Balance

Eating with Awareness

As we've learned, teenage girls and young women are developing worrying mental health issue in higher numbers than ever before. My professional work in diagnosing and treating psychological disorders in teens and young women has never been more necessary. Young women are drowning in videos and photos on social media that portray the perfect body and lifestyle as a realistic and attainable ambition. This can lead to—amongst other issues—body dissatisfaction and eating disorders.

Combined with our always-on lives, hectic schedules and busy lifestyles often dictate our eating habits, meaning it's easy to fall into the trap of mindless eating. Rushing through meals, snacking on the go, and consuming processed convenience foods can lead to disconnected eating patterns and imbalanced nutrition. However, by embracing the practice of mindful eating and prioritising nutrition that supports Chi balance, we can cultivate a deeper connection with our bodies, enhance our overall wellbeing, and harmonise our energy flow.

Mindful eating is a holistic approach to nourishment that involves bringing conscious awareness to the entire eating experience, from food selection and preparation to the act of eating itself. By slowing down, tuning into our body's hunger and fullness cues, and savouring each bite mindfully, we can create a more mindful relationship with food and cultivate greater balance in our Chi energy.

In this section, we'll explore the principles of mindful eating and nutrition for Chi balance, including techniques for cultivating awareness, selecting Chi-enhancing foods, and honouring the body's wisdom. By incorporating these practices into our daily lives, we can transform our relationship with food, support our Chi energy flow, and enhance our overall health and vitality.

Practice Mindful Eating

Slow down your eating pace and savour each bite of food. Pay attention to the flavours, textures, and sensations as you chew and swallow. This mindful approach helps you appreciate the sensory experience of eating and fosters a deeper connection with your food.

Eliminate Distractions

Avoid multitasking while eating, such as watching TV, scrolling through your phone, or working on your computer. When you're distracted, you're less likely to fully enjoy your meal and may overeat without realising it. Create a peaceful dining environment free from distractions to fully focus on your food.

Emphasise Whole Foods
Base your diet on whole, minimally processed foods that are rich in nutrients. Fresh fruits, vegetables, whole grains, lean proteins, and healthy fats provide essential vitamins, minerals, antioxidants, and fibre that support overall health and vitality.

Colourful Variety
Incorporate a rainbow of colours onto your plate by including a diverse range of fruits and vegetables. Different colours indicate various phytonutrients and antioxidants, each offering unique health benefits. Aim for variety to ensure you receive a broad spectrum of nutrients to support Chi balance.

Balance Macronutrients
Include a balance of macronutrients—carbohydrates, proteins, and fats—in your meals to provide sustained energy and satiety. Choose complex carbohydrates like whole grains and legumes, lean proteins such as poultry, fish, tofu, or beans, and healthy fats like avocado, nuts, seeds, and olive oil.

Understanding Yin and Yang Foods
In Traditional Chinese Medicine, foods are categorised based on their energetic properties of Yin (cooling, nourishing) and Yang (warming, energising). Balancing these energies in your diet promotes Chi harmony and overall wellbeing.

Incorporate Yin Foods
Include cooling Yin foods like leafy greens, cucumbers, melons, berries, and sprouts to nourish and hydrate the body. These foods are rich in water content and offer refreshing and revitalising properties, ideal for maintaining internal balance.

Include Yang Foods
Incorporate warming Yang foods like ginger, garlic, onions, cinnamon, chilli peppers, and root vegetables to invigorate and energise the body. These foods stimulate circulation, digestion, and metabolism, providing a sense of warmth and vitality.

Listen to Hunger Cues

Tune into your body's hunger and fullness signals to guide your eating behaviour. Eat when you're physically hungry and stop when you're comfortably satisfied. Avoid eating out of boredom, stress, or emotional triggers, and respect your body's natural cues for nourishment.

Mindful Portion Control

Practice portion control by serving yourself reasonable portions and avoiding oversized servings. Use smaller plates and utensils to visually cue appropriate portion sizes and prevent overeating. Pay attention to your body's feedback and stop eating when you feel satisfied but not overly full.

Savour the Experience

Cultivate a mindful eating practice by savouring the entire eating experience, from meal preparation to the last bite. Engage all your senses—sight, smell, taste, touch, and even sound—to fully appreciate the sensory pleasure of eating. Chew your food slowly, chew each mouthful thoroughly, and take time to enjoy the flavours and textures.

By embracing mindful eating principles and incorporating Chi-enhancing foods into your diet, you can nourish your body, support Chi balance, and promote holistic wellbeing from within. Mindful eating cultivates a deeper connection with your body, food, and environment, fostering a sense of gratitude, presence, and vitality in your daily life.

Chi Practices for Enhancing Sleep and Rest

Quality sleep and adequate rest are essential components of overall wellbeing and vital for maintaining optimal Chi balance. However, it's no surprise that some of us struggle with sleep disturbances, insomnia, and chronic stress that disrupt our natural sleep cycles and compromise our Chi energy flow. Fortunately, by integrating Chi practices into our nightly routines and creating restful environments conducive to deep relaxation, we can enhance the quality of our sleep, restore our energy reserves, and promote Chi balance for improved physical, mental, and emotional wellbeing.

In this section, we will explore various Chi practices and techniques designed to enhance sleep and promote restorative rest. From calming bedtime rituals to soothing relaxation exercises, these practices are designed to quiet the mind, release tension from the body, and create an optimal environment for deep, rejuvenating sleep. By incorporating these Chi-enhancing practices into our nightly routines, we can harness the power of restorative rest to replenish our energy, restore balance to our Chi, and awaken each day feeling refreshed, revitalised, and ready to embrace life with renewed vitality.

Bedtime Meditation

Engaging in a calming meditation practice before bed can help quiet the mind, release stress, and prepare the body for restful sleep. Begin by finding a comfortable seated position or lying down in bed. Close your eyes and focus on your breath, inhaling deeply through your nose and exhaling slowly through your mouth. As you breathe, visualise a sense of relaxation spreading throughout your body, starting from your head and gradually flowing down to your toes. You can also incorporate soothing visualisations or repeat a calming mantra to further quiet the mind and promote relaxation.

Progressive Muscle Relaxation

This technique involves systematically tensing and relaxing different muscle groups in the body to release tension and promote relaxation. Start by lying comfortably in bed and focusing on your breath. Begin with your toes, curling them tightly for a few seconds, then releasing and allowing them to relax completely. Move on to the next muscle group, such as your calves, thighs, abdomen, chest, arms, and so on, tensing each group for a few seconds before releasing. As you progress through each muscle group, focus on the sensation of relaxation spreading throughout your body, releasing any tension or stress you may be holding onto.

Breathing Exercises

Deep breathing exercises can help calm the nervous system, reduce stress, and promote relaxation, making them an excellent practice for improving sleep quality. One effective technique is diaphragmatic breathing, also known as belly breathing. Lie comfortably in bed with one hand on your abdomen and the other on your chest. Inhale deeply through your nose, allowing your abdomen to rise as you fill your lungs with air. Exhale slowly through your mouth, feeling your abdomen fall as you release the breath. Repeat this pattern for several minutes, focusing on the sensation of your breath moving in and out of your body and allowing yourself to relax fully with each exhalation.

Guided Imagery

Guided imagery involves visualising peaceful and calming scenes or scenarios to promote relaxation and reduce stress. Before bed, close your eyes and imagine yourself in a serene natural setting, such as a tranquil beach, lush forest, or peaceful garden. Engage your senses by focusing on the sights, sounds, and sensations of this imaginary environment, allowing yourself to fully immerse in the experience. Visualise yourself feeling calm, relaxed, and at ease in this tranquil setting, letting go of any worries or tension from the day. You can also listen to guided imagery recordings or meditation apps that provide soothing visualisations and relaxation prompts to help guide you into a restful state before sleep.

Aromatherapy

Incorporating calming Essential Oils into your bedtime routine can promote relaxation, reduce stress, and improve sleep quality. Lavender, chamomile, and cedarwood are popular Essential Oils known for their calming and sedative properties. You can diffuse these oils in your bedroom before bedtime, add a few drops to a warm bath, or apply diluted oil to pulse points or the bottoms of your feet. As you inhale the soothing scent of these oils, allow yourself to relax deeply and prepare for restful sleep.

By incorporating these Chi-enhancing practices into your nightly routine, you can create a peaceful and restorative bedtime ritual that promotes deep relaxation, releases tension, and prepares your body and mind for restful sleep.

Throughout this chapter, we have explored various ways to infuse Chi into everyday activities, from mindful eating and creating harmonious living spaces to enhancing sleep and rest through Chi-inspired practices. By incorporating these techniques into your daily routines, you can cultivate a deeper sense of connection with your body, mind, and spirit, and experience greater balance, vitality, and wellbeing.

CHAPTER 13

NATURE AND ENVIRONMENTAL HARMONY

Life today can be an exhilarating and rewarding adventure, but often there's a price to pay for our always-on lifestyles. We've learned how we can regain control of our emotional and mental wellbeing through simple Chi practices and exercises, but now we need to think of the wider world, in particular the damaging effect we inadvertently have on nature and the planet.

In this chapter, we will explore the profound connection between Chi and the natural world, and how cultivating a deeper relationship with nature can enhance our overall vitality and harmony.

From the gentle rustle of leaves in the wind to the soothing sound of flowing water, Chi, nature's energy, surrounds us in every moment. By reconnecting with the earth's natural rhythms and immersing ourselves in the healing energy of the natural world, we can tap into a limitless source of vitality and inspiration.

Connecting with Nature's Chi

We're more connected today than humans have ever been. We're never away from our phones; we're bombarded with social media posts from influencers who claim to have the perfect life, and we're exposed to more glamorous beauty advertising than ever. Unfortunately, despite being always connected through technology and brand advertising, it's easy to become disconnected from the natural world and the vital energy it provides.

Re-establishing a connection with nature's Chi can have profound benefits for our physical, mental, and emotional wellbeing. To truly connect with nature's Chi, we must first cultivate mindfulness and presence in our interactions with the natural world.

One powerful way to connect with nature's Chi is through mindful walks in natural settings such as parks, forests, or along the seashore. As we walk, we can bring our attention to the sights, sounds, and sensations of the environment around us. We can observe the intricate patterns of leaves, the gentle sway of branches in the wind, and the rhythmic ebb and flow of waves. By immersing ourselves in nature's beauty and presence, we can begin to align ourselves with its natural rhythms and absorb its healing energy.

Another powerful practice for connecting with nature's Chi is grounding or earthing, which involves direct physical contact with the earth's surface. Whether it's walking barefoot on grass or soil, lying on the ground, or sitting against a tree, grounding allows us to absorb the earth's energy directly into our bodies. This simple practice can help reduce inflammation, improve sleep, and promote a sense of calm and wellbeing.

Additionally, spending time in natural settings such as parks, gardens, or wilderness areas can provide opportunities for relaxation, rejuvenation, and reflection. Whether it's enjoying a picnic in the park, practicing yoga outdoors, or simply sitting quietly and listening to the sounds of nature, spending time in natural environments can help us recharge our energy reserves and reconnect with our inner selves.

By consciously cultivating a deeper connection with nature's Chi, we can tap into a limitless source of vitality and inspiration. Whether it's through mindful walks, grounding practices, or simply spending time in natural settings, connecting with nature's Chi can help us restore balance, reduce stress, and enhance our overall sense of wellbeing.

As we continue to explore the profound connection between Chi and the natural world, let us remember to approach our interactions with nature with reverence, gratitude, and humility. By honouring the sacredness of the natural world and recognising our interconnectedness with all living beings, we can deepen our connection with nature's Chi and experience its transformative power in our lives.

In our modern, technology-driven lives, it's easy to become disconnected from the natural world and the vital energy it provides. However, reestablishing a connection with nature's Chi can have profound benefits for our physical, mental, and emotional wellbeing. To truly connect with nature's Chi, we must first cultivate mindfulness and presence in our interactions with the natural world.

One powerful way to connect with nature's Chi is through mindful walks in natural settings such as parks, forests, or along the seashore. As we walk, we can bring our attention to the sights, sounds, and sensations of the environment around us. We can observe the intricate patterns of leaves, the gentle sway of branches in the wind, and the rhythmic ebb and flow of waves. By immersing ourselves in nature's beauty and presence, we can begin to align ourselves with its natural rhythms and absorb its healing energy.

Another powerful practice for connecting with nature's Chi is grounding or earthing, which involves direct physical contact with the earth's surface. Whether it's walking barefoot on grass or soil, lying on the ground, or sitting against a tree, grounding allows us to absorb the earth's energy directly into our bodies. This simple practice can help reduce inflammation, improve sleep, and promote a sense of calm and wellbeing.

Additionally, spending time in natural settings such as parks, gardens, or wilderness areas can provide opportunities for relaxation, rejuvenation, and reflection. Whether it's enjoying a picnic in the park, practicing yoga outdoors, or simply sitting quietly and listening to the sounds of nature, spending time in natural environments can help us recharge our energy reserves and reconnect with our inner selves.

By consciously cultivating a deeper connection with nature's Chi, we can tap into a limitless source of vitality and inspiration.

Whether it's through mindful walks, grounding practices, or simply spending time in natural settings, connecting with nature's Chi can help us restore balance, reduce stress, and enhance our overall sense of wellbeing.

As we continue to explore the profound connection between Chi and the natural world, let us remember to approach our interactions with nature with reverence, gratitude, and humility. By honouring the sacredness of the natural world and recognising our interconnectedness with all living beings, we can deepen our connection with nature's Chi and experience its transformative power in our lives.

Practices for Grounding and Earth Energy

Grounding, also known as earthing, is a practice that involves connecting directly with the Earth's surface to absorb its natural energy. In our modern lives, we often spend the majority of our time indoors, surrounded by technology and disconnected from the Earth's natural rhythms. This disconnection can lead to feelings of stress, fatigue, and imbalance. Grounding practices offer a simple yet powerful way to reconnect with the Earth and restore our natural equilibrium.

One of the most accessible grounding practices is walking barefoot on natural surfaces such as grass, soil, sand, or even concrete. When we walk barefoot, the soles of our feet come into direct contact with the Earth, allowing us to absorb its energy. This practice can be done in a backyard, park, beach, or any natural environment where it's safe to walk barefoot.

Another grounding practice is lying or sitting directly on the Earth's surface. Whether it's lying down on a patch of grass, sitting against the trunk of a tree, or reclining on a sandy beach, making physical contact with the Earth allows us to absorb its energy more effectively. This practice can be especially beneficial for calming the mind, reducing stress, and promoting relaxation.

For those who may not have access to outdoor spaces, grounding mats or sheets can be used indoors to simulate the effects of grounding. These products are typically made with conductive materials that mimic the Earth's natural energy, allowing individuals to experience the benefits of grounding even when indoors.

In addition to direct physical contact with the Earth, grounding practices can also involve visualisation and meditation techniques. One simple visualisation is imagining roots extending from the soles of your feet deep into the Earth, anchoring you to its energy. This visualisation can help you feel more grounded, centred, and connected to the Earth's natural rhythms.

Meditation practices can also incorporate grounding techniques by focusing on the sensations of the body in contact with the Earth. By bringing attention to the feeling of your feet touching the ground or the weight of your body pressing against the Earth, you can cultivate a deeper sense of connection and presence.

Overall, grounding practices offer a powerful way to reconnect with the Earth's energy and restore balance to our bodies and minds. Whether through walking barefoot, lying on the ground, using grounding products, or practicing visualisation and meditation, incorporating grounding into our daily routines can help us feel more grounded, centred, and connected to the Earth's natural rhythms.

Forest Bathing and Chi Healing

Forest bathing, or shinrin-yoku in Japanese, is a practice that involves immersing oneself in nature, particularly in forests, for the purpose of promoting health and wellbeing. Originating in Japan in the 1980s, forest bathing has gained popularity worldwide as a therapeutic practice for reducing stress, boosting mood, and enhancing overall health.

The practice of forest bathing is rooted in the belief that spending time in natural environments, particularly forests, can have profound healing effects on the mind, body, and spirit. Forests are rich in phytoncides, which are natural compounds released by trees and plants. These phytoncides have been shown to have antimicrobial properties and can help boost the immune system, reduce inflammation, and promote relaxation.

Forest bathing involves engaging all five senses to fully immerse oneself in the forest environment. Participants are encouraged to take slow, mindful walks through the forest, paying close attention to the sights, sounds, smells, textures, and tastes of the natural surroundings. By slowing down and being fully present in the forest, individuals can experience a profound sense of connection with nature and tap into its healing energies.

One of the key aspects of forest bathing is the practice of mindfulness, or being fully present in the moment without judgment. Mindful forest walks involve walking slowly and deliberately, taking time to observe and appreciate the beauty of the forest, and tuning into the sensations of the body and breath.

Another aspect of forest bathing is the practice of deep breathing and conscious relaxation. Participants are encouraged to take deep, slow breaths and to consciously relax their bodies as they walk through the forest. This deep breathing helps to oxygenate the body, reduce stress, and promote a sense of calm and relaxation.

Forest bathing can also include specific healing exercises or meditations designed to enhance the healing effects of the forest environment. These exercises may involve visualisations, affirmations, or energy healing techniques aimed at clearing blockages, balancing energy, and promoting overall wellbeing.

Overall, forest bathing offers a powerful way to connect with nature and harness its healing energies for physical, emotional, and spiritual wellbeing. By immersing oneself in the natural beauty of the forest, practicing mindfulness and deep breathing, and engaging in healing exercises, individuals can experience profound relaxation, rejuvenation, and renewal.

Environmental Awareness and Chi Preservation

In the modern world, environmental awareness has become increasingly important as we face global challenges such as climate change, pollution, deforestation, and loss of biodiversity. As stewards of the Earth, it is essential for us to cultivate a deeper understanding of our interconnectedness with the natural world and to take action to protect and preserve the planet for future generations.

Chi preservation is closely linked to environmental awareness, as the health and vitality of our planet directly impact the flow of

Chi, or life energy, in the world around us. When the natural environment is healthy and balanced, Chi flows freely, supporting the wellbeing of all living beings. However, when the environment is degraded or polluted, the flow of Chi becomes disrupted, leading to imbalances and disharmony.

One of the key principles of Chi preservation is the concept of living in harmony with nature. This involves adopting sustainable practices that minimise our impact on the environment and promote the health and vitality of natural ecosystems. By reducing our carbon footprint, conserving resources, and supporting renewable energy sources, we can help preserve the Earth's natural balance and protect the flow of Chi.

Environmental awareness also involves recognising the interconnectedness of all living beings and ecosystems. Just as each individual is part of a larger community, every species and habitat plays a unique role in the web of life. When we understand and respect this interconnectedness, we are more likely to make choices that support the health and wellbeing of the entire planet.

Another aspect of environmental awareness is the importance of conservation and habitat protection. By preserving natural habitats and protecting endangered species, we can help maintain biodiversity and ensure the resilience of ecosystems. This, in turn, supports the flow of Chi and contributes to the overall health and balance of the planet.

Education and advocacy are also essential components of environmental awareness and Chi preservation. By raising awareness about environmental issues, advocating for policies that protect the environment, and supporting organisations and initiatives that promote sustainability, we can help create positive change on both local and global scales.

Ultimately, environmental awareness and Chi preservation are about recognising our responsibility as caretakers of the Earth and taking action to protect and preserve the natural world for future generations. By cultivating a deeper connection with nature, adopting sustainable practices, and advocating for environmental protection, we can help ensure a healthy and vibrant planet for all beings.

In conclusion, this chapter has taken us on a journey into the heart of nature, exploring the transformative power of connecting with the Earth's Chi. Each section has illuminated the intricate relationship between individuals and the environment, emphasising the need for balance and harmony in our interconnected world.

Connecting with Nature's Chi opened our eyes to the profound energy that surrounds us, encouraging practices that align our beings with the natural rhythms of the Earth. Grounding techniques reminded us of the simplicity and effectiveness of reconnecting with the earth's energy to find stability in our fast-paced lives.

Forest Bathing and Chi Healing introduced us to the therapeutic wonders of the forest, demonstrating how nature's embrace can heal both body and soul. The exploration of Environmental Awareness and Chi Preservation underscored the urgency of protecting our planet, acknowledging that the preservation of Chi is not only a personal but a collective responsibility.

As we conclude this chapter, it is clear that integrating nature and environmental harmony into our lives is not just a choice but a necessity for wellbeing. By embracing these principles, we not only enhance our individual Chi but contribute to the overall balance of the world. As we move forward, let us carry the lessons of this chapter, fostering a deep connection with nature and a commitment to preserving the Chi that sustains us all.

CHAPTER 14

COMMUNITY AND COLLECTIVE CHI

Let's explore the transformative power of community and collective Chi, emphasising the importance of connection and collaboration in our journey towards holistic wellbeing. As social beings, humans thrive in community, drawing strength and support from shared experiences and collective endeavours. This chapter explores how fostering Chi communities, engaging in group practices, and participating in collaborative projects can not only enhance individual Chi but also contribute to the collective healing and empowerment of society. Through the exploration of various sub-sections, we will uncover the profound impact of community and collective Chi on personal growth, social cohesion, and the greater good. Let us embark on this journey together, as we discover the power of community in nurturing and sustaining our Chi.

Creating Chi Communities and Support Networks

In a world where individualism often takes precedence, the importance of community and support networks cannot be overstated. Building and nurturing Chi communities and support networks provide a vital foundation for personal growth, resilience, and wellbeing. These networks offer a safe space for individuals to share experiences, exchange knowledge, and provide mutual support, fostering a sense of belonging and interconnectedness.

One of the key aspects of creating Chi communities is fostering an environment of inclusivity and acceptance. Chi communities welcome individuals from all walks of life, regardless of background, ethnicity, gender, or belief system. By embracing diversity and celebrating the unique gifts and perspectives of each member, Chi communities create a rich tapestry of collective wisdom and experience.

Support networks within Chi communities serve as a lifeline for individuals facing challenges or navigating transitions in their lives. Whether it's offering emotional support during difficult times, providing practical assistance in times of need, or simply lending a listening ear, support networks play a crucial role in helping individuals feel seen, heard, and valued.

Furthermore, Chi communities and support networks serve as catalysts for personal growth and transformation. By engaging in regular interactions with like-minded individuals who share similar goals and aspirations, members of Chi communities can draw inspiration, motivation, and encouragement from one another. These interactions foster a culture of continuous learning and growth, empowering individuals to realise their full potential and pursue their dreams with confidence and determination.

Additionally, Chi communities provide a platform for collaboration and collective action. By coming together to address common challenges or pursue shared goals, members of Chi communities can amplify their impact and effect positive change on a larger scale. Whether it's organising community events, advocating for social causes, or initiating collaborative projects, Chi communities harness the collective energy and resources of their members to create meaningful and lasting impact in their communities and beyond.

Chi Circles and Group Practices

Chi Circles are gatherings of individuals who come together with the intention of deepening their understanding and practice of Chi. These circles provide a supportive and collaborative environment where participants can engage in various Chi practices, share insights, and cultivate a sense of connection and community.

One of the key features of Chi Circles is their emphasis on experiential learning and practice. Participants engage in a variety of Chi practices, such as breathwork, meditation, energy healing, and movement exercises, guided by experienced facilitators or practitioners. Through hands-on experience and guided exploration, participants deepen their understanding of Chi principles and techniques, cultivating greater awareness, presence, and vitality.

Moreover, Chi Circles offer a space for individuals to connect with like-minded peers and share their experiences and insights on their Chi journey. Participants often engage in group discussions, sharing their personal experiences, challenges, and breakthroughs, and offering support and encouragement to one another. This collective sharing of wisdom and knowledge creates a sense of camaraderie and mutual support among participants, fostering a strong sense of community and belonging.

Additionally, Chi Circles provide a platform for collective healing and transformation. By coming together in a supportive and energetically charged environment, participants can tap into the collective Chi field and amplify their individual healing intentions and practices. This collective synergy enhances the efficacy of individual practices, facilitating deeper healing and transformation on physical, emotional, and spiritual levels.

Furthermore, Chi Circles often incorporate rituals and ceremonies to honour the natural cycles and rhythms of life and to deepen participants' connection to the larger web of life. These rituals may include ceremonies to mark significant life transitions, seasonal celebrations to align with the cycles of nature, or ceremonial practices to cultivate gratitude and reverence for the interconnectedness of all beings.

Collaborative Chi Projects for Social Impact

Collaborative Chi Projects harness the collective power of Chi to create positive change and social impact in communities and beyond. These projects bring together individuals, organisations, and communities to collaborate on initiatives that promote wellbeing, resilience, and empowerment, while also addressing social, environmental, and humanitarian challenges.

One of the key features of Collaborative Chi Projects is their focus on co-creation and collective action. Participants from diverse backgrounds and expertise come together to identify pressing issues and co-design innovative solutions grounded in Chi principles and practices. By pooling their resources, skills, and energy, collaborators leverage the power of synergy to amplify their impact and create meaningful change.

Moreover, Collaborative Chi Projects often incorporate principles of holistic wellbeing and sustainability into their initiatives. Projects may focus on areas such as health and wellness, education, environmental conservation, social justice, and community development, aiming to address interconnected challenges and promote holistic flourishing for individuals and communities.

Additionally, Collaborative Chi Projects foster a culture of collaboration, inclusivity, and empowerment. Participants engage in open dialogue, shared decision-making, and participatory processes, honouring diverse perspectives and co-creating solutions that resonate with the needs and aspirations of all stakeholders. By fostering a sense of ownership and agency among participants, these projects empower individuals and communities to take proactive steps towards positive change and collective flourishing.

Furthermore, Collaborative Chi Projects often integrate traditional wisdom, cultural practices, and indigenous knowledge into their initiatives, honouring diverse cultural heritage and promoting cultural resilience and vitality. By drawing on the wisdom of diverse cultures and traditions, these projects enrich their interventions and create culturally relevant and inclusive solutions that resonate with local communities.

In summary, Collaborative Chi Projects harness the collective power of Chi to address pressing social, environmental, and humanitarian challenges while promoting wellbeing, resilience, and empowerment. By fostering collaboration, inclusivity, and co-creation, these projects empower individuals and communities to create positive change and contribute to a more just, sustainable, and compassionate world.

Collective Healing and Empowerment through Chi

Collective Healing and Empowerment through Chi represents a transformative journey of healing and empowerment that individuals and communities embark on together, drawing on the healing power of Chi to address collective trauma, foster resilience, and promote holistic wellbeing. This sub-section explores the profound potential of Chi practices to facilitate collective healing and empowerment on both personal and communal levels.

At its core, Collective Healing and Empowerment through Chi acknowledges the interconnectedness of individual and collective wellbeing and recognises the significance of addressing shared wounds and traumas within communities. By cultivating a collective space for healing and empowerment, individuals come together to support one another in their healing journeys, fostering a sense of solidarity, belonging, and shared purpose.

One of the key elements of Collective Healing and Empowerment through Chi is the creation of safe and nurturing spaces where individuals can come together to share their experiences, express their emotions, and engage in healing practices collectively. These spaces, whether physical or virtual, provide a supportive environment where participants feel seen, heard, and validated, fostering a sense of connection and community.

Moreover, Collective Healing and Empowerment through Chi often involves the integration of various Chi practices and modalities that promote healing and resilience on physical, emotional, mental, and spiritual levels. These may include practices such as meditation, breathwork, mindfulness, energy healing, movement therapy, expressive arts, and ritual ceremonies, among others. By engaging in these practices collectively, participants tap into the healing power of Chi to release stagnant energy, process emotions, and cultivate inner peace and balance.

Furthermore, Collective Healing and Empowerment through Chi emphasises the importance of collective rituals and ceremonies as powerful tools for healing, transformation, and community building. These rituals, which may include ceremonies such as group meditations, energy healing circles, sound baths, and sacred ceremonies, serve as potent vehicles for collective intention-setting, energy amplification, and shared healing experiences.

Additionally, Collective Healing and Empowerment through Chi recognises the role of community activism and social justice in collective healing and empowerment. By addressing systemic injustices, promoting equity, and advocating for positive social change, communities harness the transformative power of Chi to create more just, inclusive, and compassionate societies, where all individuals can thrive and flourish.

In conclusion, this chapter has explored the profound potential of Chi in fostering community and collective wellbeing through various sub-sections, each highlighting different aspects of this transformative journey. From creating supportive Chi communities and networks to engaging in group practices and collaborative projects for social impact, the chapter has emphasised the importance of collective healing, empowerment, and social justice.

Creating Chi Communities and Support Networks delved into the significance of building safe and nurturing spaces where individuals can come together to share experiences, express emotions, and engage in healing practices collectively. These communities provide a sense of solidarity, belonging, and shared purpose, fostering connection and mutual support among members.

Chi Circles and Group Practices highlighted the power of collective rituals and ceremonies as vehicles for healing, transformation, and community building. Through practices such as group meditations, energy healing circles, and sacred ceremonies, participants tap into the healing power of Chi to amplify intentions, release stagnant energy, and cultivate inner peace and balance.

Collaborative Chi Projects for Social Impact explored the role of community activism and social justice in collective healing and empowerment. By addressing systemic injustices and advocating for positive social change, communities harness the transformative power of Chi to create more just, inclusive, and compassionate societies where all individuals can thrive.

Finally, Collective Healing and Empowerment through Chi brought together the themes of collective healing and empowerment, emphasising the interconnectedness of individual and communal wellbeing. By engaging in practices that promote healing on physical, emotional, mental, and spiritual levels, communities embark on a transformative journey of resilience, empowerment, and social change.

In essence, this chapter has underscored the transformative potential of Chi in fostering community and collective wellbeing, highlighting the importance of creating supportive networks, engaging in group practices, advocating for social justice, and harnessing the healing power of Chi to create a more just, compassionate, and empowered world for all.

CHAPTER 14

PERSONAL STORIES OF CHI TRANSFORMATION

Our journey takes us to the final chapter for now, where we dive into the inspiring world of personal stories showcasing the transformative power of Chi. Throughout this chapter, we will explore real-life narratives of individuals who have embarked on profound journeys of growth, healing, and empowerment through their engagement with Chi practices. From overcoming challenges and cultivating resilience to experiencing profound shifts in health and wellbeing, these stories offer a glimpse into the diverse ways in which Chi has touched and transformed lives. Through firsthand accounts and testimonials, we gain insight into the deeply personal and impactful nature of Chi in the lives of individuals from all walks of life.

Chi Journeys of Personal Growth and Transformation

In this section, we embark on a journey through personal narratives that illuminate the profound impact of Chi on individual growth and transformation. Each story is a testament to the power of Chi to inspire positive change, foster personal development, and guide individuals towards a path of greater self-awareness and fulfilment.

Embracing Self-Discovery
These stories often begin with a moment of introspection or a realisation that prompts individuals to seek deeper meaning and purpose in their lives. Whether it's through meditation, breathwork, or other Chi practices, many find themselves drawn to explore the depths of their inner being, uncovering hidden talents, passions, and insights along the way.

Overcoming Obstacles
Life's challenges can sometimes feel insurmountable, but Chi offers a source of strength and resilience that enables individuals to face adversity with courage and determination. Through practices such as mindfulness, Acupressure, and energy healing, many have discovered a newfound sense of empowerment that allows them to navigate life's obstacles with grace and resilience.

Cultivating Inner Harmony
Central to many Chi journeys is the cultivation of inner harmony and balance. By aligning mind, body, and spirit, individuals are able to experience a profound sense of peace, clarity, and wellbeing. Through practices such as meditation, yoga, and mindful movement, many have found a deep sense of inner calm and serenity that permeates every aspect of their lives.

Awakening to Purpose
As individuals deepen their connection to Chi, they often find themselves awakening to a greater sense of purpose and meaning in life. Whether it's through serving others, pursuing creative passions, or contributing to the greater good, many discover a sense of fulfilment and purpose that guides them towards a more meaningful and purposeful existence.

Embracing Transformation
Ultimately, the stories shared in this sub-section are a celebration of transformation and growth. Through their engagement with Chi practices, individuals have experienced profound shifts in their lives, from overcoming personal challenges and limiting beliefs to embracing their true potential and stepping into their

power. These stories serve as a powerful reminder of the transformative power of Chi and its capacity to guide us towards a life of greater purpose, joy, and fulfilment.

Testimonials of Chi Practices in Daily Life

In this section, we take a peek into the real-life experiences and testimonials of young women who have incorporated Chi practices into their daily lives. From unexpected encounters to transformative moments, these stories offer a glimpse into the diverse ways in which Chi has made a profound impact on their wellbeing, relationships, and overall outlook on life.

Sarah's Serendipitous Encounter
Sarah, a 26-year-old marketing executive, stumbled upon Chi during a particularly stressful period at work. Intrigued by its potential to alleviate stress and promote wellbeing, she decided to explore Chi through daily meditation and mindfulness practices. What started as a simple experiment soon became a transformative journey, as Sarah discovered a newfound sense of calm and clarity that permeated every aspect of her life. From navigating challenging meetings with ease to fostering deeper connections with colleagues, Chi became her secret weapon for success in the fast-paced world of marketing.

Emily's Journey to Self-Discovery
Emily, a 23-year-old college student, embarked on a journey of self-discovery after experiencing a series of setbacks in her personal life. Seeking solace and guidance, she turned to Chi practices such as yoga and breathwork, finding refuge in the gentle rhythm of her breath and the grounding presence of her mat. Through consistent practice, Emily not only found relief from anxiety and stress but also discovered a newfound sense of self-awareness and inner strength. From passing her exams with relative ease to forging deeper connections with friends and family, Chi became her anchor in navigating the ups and downs of college life.

Ava's Quest for Balance

Ava, a 29-year-old entrepreneur, struggled to find balance amidst the demands of running her own business and caring for her young family. Determined to prioritise her wellbeing, she turned to Chi practices such as Acupressure and energy healing to restore balance and harmony in her life. Through regular self-care rituals and mindfulness practices, Ava not only found relief from stress and overwhelm but also discovered a newfound sense of vitality and purpose. From juggling deadlines to fostering deeper connections with her loved ones, Chi became her guiding light in navigating the complexities of modern-day entrepreneurship.

Shelly's Healing Journey

Shelly, a 30-year-old artist, embarked on a healing journey after experiencing a period of profound loss and grief in her life. Seeking solace and healing, she turned to Chi practices such as Aromatherapy and meditation to soothe her heart and nourish her soul. Through the therapeutic power of Essential Oils and guided meditation, Shelly not only found relief from emotional pain but also discovered a newfound sense of peace and resilience. From channeling her grief into creative expression to finding solace in nature's embrace, Chi became her lifeline in navigating the depths of her emotions and embracing the journey of healing and transformation.

Olivia's Journey to Empowerment

Olivia, a 27-year-old activist and speaker, embarked on a journey of empowerment after witnessing the impact of Chi practices on her physical and mental wellbeing. Inspired by the transformative power of mindfulness and energy healing, she began integrating Chi into her daily routine, using it as a tool for self-care and resilience in the face of adversity. From organising community events to advocating for social change, Olivia found renewed strength and purpose in her activism, fuelled by the empowering practices of Chi. From overcoming burnout to fostering collective healing within her community, Chi became her guiding force in creating positive change and empowering others to do the same.

Isabella's Journey to Inner Peace

Isabella, a 19-year-old introverted student, embarked on a journey to find inner peace amidst the chaos of academic pressure and personal challenges. Turning to Chi practices such as meditation and journaling, she discovered a sanctuary within herself where she could retreat and find solace. Through the practice of mindfulness and self-reflection, Izzy not only found relief from stress and anxiety but also cultivated a deep sense of inner peace and serenity. From passing her entrance exams with confidence to navigating personal relationships with ease, Chi became her anchor in the turbulent waters of student life.

Grace's Journey to Radiant Health

Grace, a 26-year-old graphic designer, embarked on a journey to radiant health after experiencing poor health and low energy after a period of unemployment. Seeking holistic solutions to support her wellbeing, she turned to Chi practices to nourish her body and revitalise her energy. Through the power of mindful eating and energy cleansing rituals, Grace not only restored balance and vitality to her body but also cultivated a deep sense of gratitude and appreciation for her health. From fuelling her body with nutrient-dense foods to cleansing her energy with daily rituals, Chi became her guiding force in achieving radiant health and vitality.

Daisy's Quest for Spiritual Growth

Daisy, a 28-year-old plus size model embarked on a quest for spiritual growth and enlightenment after experiencing a deep longing for connection and purpose in her life after years of bullying. Turning to Chi practices such as meditation and energy healing, she embarked on a journey of self-discovery and inner transformation. Through the practice of Aromatherapy, meditation and energy healing, Daisy not only found solace and guidance but also discovered a profound sense of connection to the universe and the divine within herself. From communing with nature to exploring sacred rituals, Chi became her sacred companion in the journey of spiritual growth and enlightenment.

Harper's Journey to Empowered Creativity

Harper, a 25-year-old artist, embarked on a journey to reclaim their creative power and express themselves authentically through their art. Turning to Chi practices such as Aromatherapy and visualisation techniques, they tapped into their inner reservoir of creativity and inspiration. Through the therapeutic power of Essential Oils and visualisation, Harper not only found inspiration and clarity but also discovered a newfound sense of confidence and empowerment in their artistic endeavours. From channeling their emotions into their artwork to sharing their creations with the world, Chi became their muse and guiding light in the journey of empowered creativity and self-expression.

Ava's Path to Emotional Resilience

Ava, 23-year-old law graduate, embarked on a path to emotional resilience after facing setbacks and challenges in her career and personal life. Turning to Chi practices such as breathwork, mindfulness and journaling, she found solace and strength in moments of adversity. Through the power of mindfulness and journaling, Ava not only gained clarity and perspective but also developed a resilient mindset that helped her navigate life's ups and downs with grace and resilience. From thriving in her professional endeavours to fostering deeper connections in her personal relationships, Chi became her anchor in the journey of emotional resilience and growth.

Authentic Stories of Chi Empowerment and Resilience

With the permission of my beautiful, brave friends and clients, here are some of their own personal stories of adversity, hope, stress, failure, success and ultimately finding inner strength from Chi. Names have been changed to protect the superstars.

Navigating the Unknown: Bobbi's Illuminated Path to Self-Discovery

Bobbi never knew what she wanted to be when she grew up. She was smart at school and never in any trouble. She got great grades and applied to University to study International Business.

"Business Studies courses are full of people that want to be successful but most don't know what they want to be successful at", she said. "I hoped that I'd find out what I wanted to do at some point before I graduated".

Three years into her course, Bobbi got disillusioned with how her life was panning out. She had a distinct lack of clarity about her future vocation and this began to drain her enthusiasm. "I was despairing that I'd made a big mistake with my life choices and I needed a way out".

If you believe in luck then you're probably attuned to the powers of inner life forces and fate. And as fate would have it, Bobbi found herself in her final year internship at an Advertising Agency, spending three months working in various departments, from Account Management to Data Science and Media Planning.

"There was a large chill-out area in the Agency where everyone would hang out at lunchtime and read magazines or just put their headphones on and tune out. I was alone—as usual—and picked up a random women's magazine one day and read an article about Chi and inner life-forces. I'd never heard of Chi but it sounded amazing and made me curious. I read that we all have an inner life force, called Chi, that can be nurtured and strengthened. I've never been a particularly spiritual person but it all began to make sense—my lack of ambition, apathy towards Uni and just a general feeling of 'meh' was all down to my Chi being messed up".

Determined to see if this was the secret answer she'd been looking for, Bobbi threw herself in a Chi lifestyle. She learned how to control her self-doubt and figured out how to focus on herself and her future, blocking out the negativity that was making her confused, unclear and anxious.

"I changed my daily routine to include Chi practices like deep breathing exercises, meditation and relaxation. I incorporated Aromatherapy products into my me-time and I stopped doing all those toxic little things like snoozing my alarm 10 times every morning, eating girl dinners instead of healthy food and biggest of all for me, I actually got dressed at the weekend instead of slobbing in my pyjamas the whole time".

Bobbi says it didn't take long for these little changes to take effect. After graduating, she found her place in the Communication industry at a top PR company, advising clients on their marketing strategies.

"I practice Chi every single day, it's now just part of who I am and I feel so much more focussed and ambitious. I love my job and it's hard to believe that a couple of years ago I had no idea what I wanted be".

Believe + Achieve: Evie's Awakening to the Powers of Chi

Evie was 21 when she found herself haunted with a sense of aimlessness and disillusionment. Once full of passion and creativity, Evie found herself adrift in a sea of nothingness. Each day blurred into the next, a monotonous cycle of uninspiring tasks and unfulfilled potential.

Evie dropped out of her University course and her dreams of a career in Fashion Design faded into the background as she languished in a dead-end job.

"I tried to tell myself the crappy job was temporary, and that I'd be back to normal soon, but the reality was, I didn't even know where to start. My mum and dad didn't even know I'd left Uni and didn't know I was feeling so low and worthless".

Finally, Evie decided enough was enough and started her journey of recovery after being inspired by a podcast about Chi. Evie realised her inner life force was the answer.

"To be honest, I knew my spirit was so down it was practically asleep. Discovering Chi was a game-changing moment for me and I felt better almost as soon as I started a self-care routine."

Evie introduced Aromatherapy, breathwork and facial massage into her morning and evening cleansing routine.

"I incorporate mood-enhancing facial products and they give me confidence and determination. I'm feeling positive and I can see through the fog now. I'm back at Uni for my final year and I'm determined to see this through and find my true purpose in life. I've started freelancing and my side hustle is making money. Who knows, this could become something amazing".

Quiet No More: Mia's Journey from Shy to Shine

To say Mia was shy would be an understatement. Mia says she was once the kind of girl that nobody noticed because she was so quiet and unassuming. That's probably OK for a tween Goth, but once Mia started out on her working life, she realised she'd need to step up, come out of the shadows and be ready to stand up and be counted. She just didn't know how to.

"I was painfully shy and painfully anxious in social situations —everything felt painful" she recalls. "When I was a young kid, my parents divorced and I think I rebelled. I was told to shut up a lot by adults and I think that imprinted some kind of trauma in me".

Things started to improve for Mia's confidence when she got her first job in a clothing store, where she was hired in the stock room. "It suited me to be alone in the background, folding clothes and unpacking deliveries with my headphones on," she says. "I didn't have to interact with strangers or make small talk with my co-workers."

One day, the store was short-staffed and Mia was asked to help at the service counter, dealing with customer returns and complaints. A particularly angry Karen, who demanded a refund on a dress she'd clearly worn was the catalyst for change for Mia. "She wouldn't let me speak and ranted at me and made me feel so small and worthless that I cried for days. It brought back my childhood trauma of being told by adults to shut up. I thought she was the worst person in the world but my manager said to get over it as it happens all the time. I finally realised that maybe I was the problem. I had no resilience to confrontation, no strength to stand up for myself and absolutely no self-control of my emotions. This neurotic, angry Karen wasn't the emotional mess, it was me. That's when I decided to improve my life and my self-worth".

Mia started with anxiety-reducing breathwork and meditation, along with therapeutic treats like uplifting Essential Oils in a hot relaxing bath, moving onto Acupressure and Aromatherapy. Along the way, Mia learned more about Chi and how our moods, emotions and general wellbeing are affected if our Chi is blocked by negative energy and stress.

"It's true what they say, the more stressed you are, the more stressed you become. Learning Chi practices really helped me visualise my problems and develop strategies to overcome them. If you can see the problem, you can fix it, but my problems started because I couldn't see how introverted I actually was. I didn't ever want to be the super loud girl but I also didn't want to be so quiet that I may as well not be there".

Six months on, Mia has made a remarkable transformation. "Life is so much more fun when you're not scared of speaking up or being noticed", she says. "Embracing Chi has given me confidence and I've also found that I want to help my friends come out of their shells too. I'm still probably nerdy and quiet compared to girls I see on Instagram, but I'm totally OK with that".

Fateful Encounters: Jaz's Serendipitous Path to Renewal

For Jaz, now 25, weekends were once a refuge, a sanctuary from the demands of the workweek. Yet even in the comfort of her own home, Jaz felt a profound sense of emptiness. Pyjama-clad and cocooned in the solitude of her flatshare, she found solace in the familiarity of her surroundings, yet yearned for something more, a spark to reignite the flame of passion that once burned brightly within her.

As the weeks turned into months, Jaz's world shrank, her social circle dwindled as she withdrew into herself, consumed by self-doubt and inertia. The thought of Monday morning filled her with dread, a relentless reminder of the grind she had grown accustomed to yet yearned to escape.

It was in the depths of this despair that Jaz's journey of self-discovery began. A chance encounter at an Aromatherapy stall at a quiet craft market in her home city led her down an unexpected path of exploration and renewal.

"The woman running the stall was lovely. I truly believe she could see instantly the problems building inside me, even though I couldn't. She handed me a home-made facial oil blended with Aromatherapy and told me to breath it in every day—as deep as I could—and hold it in for four seconds. It smelled amazing—natural, fresh, but also unlike anything I've ever smelled before.

Even now, that smell takes me back to that moment that changed everything for me", Jaz remembers.

Jaz says she felt something happen in that moment, a tiny sign that this new feeling of energy she had was something she wanted to explore further.

"I bought the oil and rushed home to use it. In fact, I sniffed it on the bus on the way home and each time it felt like my worries were slowly clearing. I used it in the bath, mixed it with my moisturiser, poured some into a hot facial spa I made with a towel over my head leaning over the sink. I used it in every way I could think of. I definitely got my money's worth from that first bottle!"

Jaz threw herself into learning more about the secret life force inside all of us, learning all the ways we can introduce mindfulness and positivity into our daily routines. Jaz's collection of Aromatherapy bottles grew and she learned how different Essential Oils produce different mood-boosting effects, using lavender and rose oil to destress after a long day and frankincense and sandalwood to face the day with strength and clarity.

"I've now incorporated Chi practices into my life wholeheartedly", she says. "I understand how Chi affects everything we do every day, from what and how we eat, to how we can influence other people with our positivity. Amazingly, I'm still working at the place I used to hate, but I changed my outlook and ended up being promoted. I now tell my team about Chi and we often have mindfulness exercises together in the office".

Lost in Transition: Sofia's Struggle to Find Connection in a Foreign Land

Sofia was an outgoing teen growing up in Madrid, Spain. She made friends easily and boys seemed to like her. Her childhood and adolescence were good and she has fond memories of that happy time in her life. When Sofia moved away from home to go to university in the US, things changed for her. Away from the familiarity of her home town, she felt overwhelmed with the changes to her life. Once she had been popular and confident; now she felt out of her depth and alone.

"Everyone expects a lifestyle shock when they go to University but no one tells you that you're basically alone even though there are hundreds of people around you. I had some friends from Spain that I'd hang out with but everyone seemed to be making friends faster than me. Soon everyone knew each other and I felt more and more isolated"

Sofia was suffering from an all-too-common feeling amongst young women of not fitting into new surroundings. These feelings can be triggered by the smallest event, and can quickly grow into neuroses. Left unchecked, we become withdrawn and begin to isolate ourselves.

It starts small—we wave across the campus to people we know when once we'd run over for a chat; we politely decline an invitation to meet friends for coffee; and we hesitate to sign up for that school trip we were once so looking forward to.

Gradually these feelings can grow. Saturday nights out are less frequent but you put that down to your homework; hanging out with friends doesn't seem so much fun any more and you start to think people are talking about you behind your back.

You develop negative thoughts about people you once loved. You're irritable when mom calls you in the evening and your hour-long calls turn into a few quick minutes. You make excuses for your behaviour but you genuinely believe it's just because you're buried under so much homework. You laugh to yourself when you remember you once thought Uni was going to be one long party.

But wait... you notice that other students aren't struggling like you. When you said you were too tired to go to that gig last week, you assumed your friends were going to give it a miss too. When you hear about your friends going backstage to meet the band after the gig, you feel let down and jealous. You feel like your friends are excluding you but it is you that is excluding yourself.

You convince yourself that you're better off without friends who don't care about you and you become ambivalent to their attention. Soon they stop inviting you, then they stop talking to you. The WhatsApp groups go quiet as you realise you haven't been invited to join new ones. Things move on, you don't.

It took Sofia a three hour therapy session with me to get that story across. Unfortunately, I've heard this story a hundred times, it's far more common that you'd think. Girls and young women have unique issues to deal with and we can be emotionally delicate when familiarity changes suddenly. Sofia wasn't prepared for the anxiety and upheaval of moving from one county to another on her own at 19. She wasn't prepared for the shock of integrating into a new culture, and she wasn't prepared for the fallout when things didn't go her way.

Reflecting on this two years later on a recent Zoom call, Sofia tells me that she can't believe she was that person—"bitter", "jealous", "snappy" were her own words to describe how she felt at that time.

"I found some kind of weird comfort in being bitchy with everyone around me, even my poor mom. It was my defence mechanism and I thought this was how you deal with change. I thought I was being strong but I wasn't, I was being really weak.

My advice for Sofia at the time was simple. I told her she had bad energy that she alone could clear. We talked for hours about Chi and the benefits of a positive outlook. Sofia left with a clear understanding of Chi and a simple prescription from me highlighting where she should focus her self-care routines.

"I embraced Chi from the moment you told me about it", she says, two years on. "I discovered how to unblock my Chi through positive action—breathing techniques, meditation, Acupressure, facial massage and Aromatherapy".

"I was going through a bad time, but I came out of it better, wiser and a much stronger person. Chi practices have been part of my life ever since. I no longer feel negative to situations I can't control and I am a much more confident person because of it".

The Loneliness Paradox: Freya's Journey from Social Butterfly to Solitary Struggle

Freya was once the epitome of a social butterfly—vibrant, outgoing, and always the life of the party. At 29, she seemed to have it all: a successful career, a wide circle of friends, and an infectious zest for life. But beneath the surface, Freya was grappling with a profound sense of guilt and grief that threatened to engulf her.

It all began with a chance encounter with a man named Alex, whose magnetic personality instantly drew Freya in. They shared a whirlwind romance, filled with laughter, adventure, and the promise of a bright future together. But tragedy struck unexpectedly when Alex passed away suddenly, leaving Freya shattered and consumed with guilt.

"I should have been there for him," Freya would whisper to herself in moments of anguish. "If only I had known…"

Her grief soon spiralled into depression, casting a shadow over every aspect of her life. Despite the outward appearance of normalcy, Freya felt like a hollow shell of her former self, trapped in a relentless cycle of guilt and despair. She withdrew from her friends, putting on a brave face during social gatherings while secretly longing for acknowledgment and understanding.

"I felt like no one truly understood what I was going through," Freya confided. "I was drowning in my own grief, and it felt like I was invisible to everyone around me."

As the days turned into weeks and months, Freya's solitary struggle became increasingly overwhelming. Despite her best efforts to maintain a facade of normalcy, the weight of her emotions threatened to crush her spirit entirely. She longed for a lifeline, a glimmer of hope to guide her out of the darkness.

It was during this time of profound introspection that Freya came across the life-giving powers of Chi. Intrigued by the concept of harnessing one's inner energy to promote healing and wellness, she immersed herself in the practice of Chi exercises and mindfulness techniques.

"I had nothing to lose," Freya recalled. "I was desperate for a way out of the darkness, and Chi seemed like my last hope."

Through dedicated practice and unwavering determination, Freya began to experience a profound transformation from within. The gentle rhythm of her breath became a source of comfort and strength, grounding her in moments of uncertainty. She embraced mindfulness meditation as a means of quieting her restless mind and finding peace amidst the chaos.

"With each breath, I felt myself letting go of the guilt and sorrow that had weighed me down for so long," Freya shared. "Chi became my anchor, guiding me back to myself and restoring my sense of purpose and vitality."

As Freya went deeper into her Chi practice, she discovered a newfound sense of resilience and inner peace. The once solitary struggle gave way to a newfound sense of connection and belonging, as she reconnected with her friends and embraced the beauty of life's journey with open arms.

"I realised that I didn't have to face my pain alone," Freya reflected. "Chi taught me that healing begins from within, and that true strength lies in the courage to embrace our vulnerabilities and seek support from those who love us."

Today, Freya's journey serves as a testament to the transformative power of Chi in overcoming adversity and finding inner peace. With each breath, she continues to navigate life's challenges with grace and resilience, guided by the boundless energy of her own Chi.

As we conclude this final chapter, we are reminded of the profound impact that Chi has had on the lives of young women from all walks of life. Through the power of mindfulness, breathwork, and self-care rituals, these stories illuminate the transformative journey of growth, healing, and empowerment that is made possible through the practice of Chi.

From overcoming challenges and cultivating resilience to experiencing profound shifts in health and wellbeing, the narratives shared in this chapter offer a glimpse into the diverse ways in which Chi has touched and transformed lives. Through firsthand accounts and testimonials, we have gained insight into the deeply personal and impactful nature of Chi in guiding individuals towards a path of greater self-awareness, fulfilment, and connection.

As we celebrate these empowering narratives of personal transformation and discovery, fuelled by the timeless wisdom and healing energy of Chi, we are reminded of the inherent power that lies within each of us to embrace our vulnerabilities, cultivate resilience, and awaken to a life of greater purpose, joy, and fulfilment.

FINAL THOUGHTS

As we come to the end of our journey together, let me take a moment to remind you that your journey is just beginning. I have guided you on this first leg but now it is down to you to continue your good work. Remember, it is important that you don't abandon your journey. It's OK to rest, but an unfinished journey is no better than no journey at all.

Life's full of ups and downs, good and bad, Yin and Yang. But each moment holds its own lesson, its own chance for growth and transformation. Remember the mantra: "I either win or I learn." There's no losing in life, only discovering; no failure, only experience; no defeat, only opportunity to grow.

Be strong and believe in yourself and take these three final guiding words from me—Transform, Thrive and Win.

Transform the knowledge and wisdom you've gained into personal growth and positive change. Thrive in every moment, embracing the fullness of life with passion and purpose. And above all, Win—not in the sense of defeating others, but in the sense of realising your true potential and living your best life.

One more thing…
As I sit here in my home in Hong Kong, it's late at night, the cats are asleep and it's dark outside. Even the famous neon signs of Hong Kong are fading for another day. I've done my best with this book. I've tried to distill a lifetime of learning and experience into these pages and something just struck me. In my efforts to help you, I now know you've also helped me. Writing this book has reinforced my belief we are nothing without each other. Life is about connections—to nature, to our conscious, to the unknown mysteries of the universe, but mostly connections to each other.

Thank you for this opportunity. Take care.
R.

GLOSSARY

Acetylcholine: A neurotransmitter responsible for various cognitive functions, including learning, memory, and muscle movement.

Acupressure: A Traditional Chinese Medicine (TCM) technique involving the application of manual pressure to specific points on the body to promote relaxation, balance energy flow, and alleviate pain or discomfort.

Acupuncture: A component of Traditional Chinese Medicine involving the insertion of thin needles into specific points on the body to stimulate energy flow, relieve pain, and promote overall wellness.

Adaptogen: A natural substance, such as herbs or mushrooms, used to help the body adapt to stress and promote overall wellbeing.

Adrenaline: Also known as epinephrine, adrenaline is a hormone and neurotransmitter produced by the adrenal glands in response to stress, fear, or excitement. Adrenaline helps prepare the body for the "fight or flight" response by increasing heart rate, blood pressure, and blood flow to muscles, dilating airways to improve oxygen intake, and releasing glucose into the bloodstream for energy. It also suppresses non-essential bodily functions such as digestion and immune response temporarily.

Aikido: Japanese martial art focused on redirecting an opponent's energy, rather than directly opposing it, to self-defence and spiritual development. Techniques involve joint locks, throws, and pins.

Aldehydes: A class of organic compounds found in some Essential Oils, characterised by the presence of a carbonyl group (C=O) bonded to a hydrogen atom and an R group. Aldehydes contribute to the scent and flavour of Essential Oils and have antimicrobial and anti-inflammatory properties.

Amino Acids: Organic compounds comprising a central carbon atom bonded to a hydrogen atom, an amino group (NH2), a carboxyl group (COOH), and a variable side chain (R group). They serve as the fundamental units of proteins and are integral to various biological processes, including protein synthesis, enzyme activity, cell signalling, and structural integrity. There are 20 standard amino acids with distinct side chains that dictate their properties and functions. These can be categorised as essential, requiring dietary intake, and non-essential, which the body can synthesise internally.

Anabolism: The metabolic process in which smaller molecules are synthesised into larger, more complex molecules, requiring energy input, typically in the form of adenosine triphosphate (ATP). Anabolism involves the assembly of simple molecules such as amino acids, fatty acids, and sugars into complex compounds like proteins, lipids, and carbohydrates, which are essential for cell growth, repair, and maintenance. Enzymes play a crucial role in catalysing the anabolic reactions that occur within cells, facilitating the formation of new chemical bonds and the storage of energy in molecular structures.

Anhedonia: The inability to experience pleasure from activities that were previously enjoyable or rewarding.

Aroma profile: The unique combination of aromatic compounds present in an Essential Oil, contributing to its distinctive scent and therapeutic properties.

Aromatherapy: The therapeutic use of Essential Oils extracted from plants to promote physical, emotional, and psychological wellbeing through inhalation or topical application.

Asanas: Physical postures or poses practiced in yoga, designed to promote strength, flexibility, balance, and relaxation. Asanas are an integral part of yoga practice and often involve holding specific body positions while focusing on breath control and mindfulness. They aim to enhance physical health, mental clarity, and spiritual awareness.

Astrology: The study of the positions and movements of celestial bodies, such as stars and planets, and their influence on human affairs and natural phenomena.

Attention-Deficit/Hyperactivity Disorder (ADHD): Neurodevelopmental disorder characterised by symptoms of inattention, hyperactivity, and impulsivity that interfere with functioning and behaviour.

Autism Spectrum Disorder (ASD): A neurodevelopmental disorder characterised by challenges with social interaction, communication, and repetitive behaviours, varying in severity and presentation across individuals.

Ayurveda: A traditional system of medicine originating in India that emphasises the balance of body, mind, and spirit through diet, herbal remedies, yoga, and other holistic practices.

Bipolar Disorder: A mood disorder characterised by alternating episodes of depression and mania or hypomania, affecting mood, energy levels, and behaviour.

Biofeedback: A technique that uses electronic monitoring to provide real-time information about physiological processes, such as heart rate or muscle tension, to promote self-regulation and relaxation.

Carrier oil: A base oil used to dilute Essential Oils before topical application, helping to reduce skin sensitivity and enhance absorption of the Essential Oils.

Catabolism: The metabolic process in which larger molecules are broken down into smaller ones, releasing energy in the form of adenosine triphosphate (ATP). Catabolism involves the breakdown of complex molecules such as carbohydrates, fats, and proteins into simpler compounds, which can then be used for energy production or as building blocks for cellular processes. Enzymes play a crucial role in catalysing the catabolic reactions that occur within cells, facilitating the release of energy stored in chemical bonds.

Cellular Signalling: The process by which cells communicate to coordinate functions and responses. Signals, often chemical molecules, transmit messages between cells or from the environment to cells. This triggers various cellular responses, including changes in gene expression and cell behaviour. Dysregulation can lead to diseases.

Cerebral Cortex: The outer layer of the brain responsible for higher cognitive functions such as thought, perception, memory, and voluntary movement. It is divided into four lobes (frontal, parietal, temporal, and occipital), each with specific functions and regions dedicated to processing sensory information, motor control, language, and executive functions. The cerebral cortex plays a crucial role in integrating sensory inputs, generating motor outputs, and orchestrating complex behaviours, making it essential for human consciousness and behaviour.

Chi: A vital energy or life force that flows through the body and animates all living things, according to Traditional Chinese Medicine and philosophy.

Chinese Zodiac: A system of astrology based on a twelve-year cycle, with each year represented by an animal sign. The cycle includes Rat, Ox, Tiger, Rabbit, Dragon, Snake, Horse, Goat, Monkey, Rooster, Dog, and Pig.

Chronic Fatigue Syndrome (CFS): A complex disorder characterised by persistent fatigue, post-exertional malaise, cognitive impairment, and other symptoms that significantly impair daily functioning.

Circadian Rhythm: A natural, internal process that regulates the sleep-wake cycle and repeats roughly every 24 hours, influenced by environmental cues such as light and temperature. Controlled by the body's internal "biological clock," circadian rhythms govern various physiological processes, including hormone secretion, metabolism, and brain wave activity. Disruptions to circadian rhythms, such as shift work or jet lag, can lead to sleep disorders, mood disturbances, and impaired cognitive function.

Cognitive Behavioural Therapy (CBT): A psychotherapeutic approach that focuses on identifying and changing negative thought patterns and behaviours to improve mental health and wellbeing.

Confucianism: A philosophical and ethical system based on the teachings of Confucius (Kong Fuzi) and subsequent Confucian scholars. It emphasises moral principles, social harmony, and virtuous conduct, promoting the cultivation of personal and social virtues such as benevolence (ren), righteousness (yi), propriety (li), and filial piety (xiao). Confucianism encompasses various aspects of life, including family relationships, governance, education, and ritual practices, with an emphasis on fulfilling social roles and duties with integrity and ethical responsibility.

Cortisol: A steroid hormone produced by the adrenal glands in response to stress and as part of the body's natural circadian rhythm. Cortisol plays a crucial role in regulating metabolism, immune function, blood pressure, and stress response. It helps mobilise energy stores by increasing blood sugar levels, suppresses inflammation, and modulates the body's response to stressors. Chronic elevation of cortisol levels can have detrimental effects on health, including impaired immune function, weight gain, and mood disorders.

Daoism (Taoism): A philosophical and spiritual tradition originating in ancient China that emphasises living in harmony with the Tao, or the natural order of the universe, through simplicity, spontaneity, and non-action.

Depression: A mood disorder characterised by persistent feelings of sadness, hopelessness, and loss of interest or pleasure in activities, affecting mood, behaviour, and overall functioning.

Diffuser: A device used to disperse Essential Oils into the air, often through ultrasonic vibrations or heat, to create a pleasant aroma and promote therapeutic effects.

Dilution ratio: The proportion of Essential Oil to carrier oil used in Aromatherapy blends, typically expressed as a percentage, to ensure safe and effective application on the skin.

Dosha: In Ayurveda, one of three fundamental energies or principles (Vata, Pitta, and Kapha) believed to govern physiological and psychological functions and influence individual constitution and health.

Dopamine: A neurotransmitter involved in reward-motivated behaviour, pleasure, movement, and motivation. It plays a crucial role in the brain's reward system and is associated with addiction, motivation, and motor control.

Dynorphins: Dynorphins are endogenous opioid peptides that act as neurotransmitters in the central nervous system. They are involved in pain perception, stress response, mood regulation, and addiction. Dynorphins exert their effects by binding to opioid receptors in the brain and spinal cord.

Dysthymia: Also known as Persistent Depressive Disorder, a chronic form of depression characterised by persistent feelings of sadness, hopelessness, and low self-esteem.

Electroencephalography (EEG): EEG is a non-invasive method for recording the brain's electrical activity using electrodes placed on the scalp. By detecting voltage changes generated by neuronal activity, EEG provides insights into brain function, aiding in diagnosing neurological disorders and studying consciousness, cognition, and sleep.

Endogenous Opioids: Natural opioids produced within the body, including endorphins, enkephalins, and dynorphins. They bind to opioid receptors in the brain and spinal cord, modulating pain perception, mood, and stress responses.

Enkephalins: Enkephalins are endogenous opioids that function as neurotransmitters in the central nervous system. They play a role in pain modulation and are involved in various physiological processes, including mood regulation and stress response.

Enzymes: Enzymes are specialised proteins that accelerate chemical reactions in living organisms without being consumed. They play vital roles in metabolic processes, including digestion and energy production, by lowering the energy required for reactions to occur. Enzymes are highly specific and regulated by factors like pH and temperature, enabling precise control of biochemical transformations in cells.

Epinephrine: (See Adrenaline).

Esters: A class of organic compounds found in some Essential Oils, characterised by the presence of an oxygen atom doubly bonded to a carbon atom within the molecule. Esters contribute to the fruity, floral, and sweet aroma of Essential Oils and have calming and balancing effects in Aromatherapy.

Essential Oils: Highly concentrated plant extracts obtained through steam distillation or other methods, used in Aromatherapy for their therapeutic properties and aromatic qualities.

Extraction method: The process used to obtain Essential Oils from plant materials, such as steam distillation, cold pressing, or solvent extraction, which can affect the composition and quality of the final product.

Fatty Acids: Fatty acids are molecules with a long hydrocarbon chain and a carboxyl group at one end. They are crucial components of lipids like triglycerides and phospholipids, forming cell membranes and storing energy. Classified by chain length and double bond presence, they regulate cellular function, metabolism, and physiological processes like inflammation and gene expression. Essential fatty acids, like omega-3 and omega-6, must be obtained from the diet.

Feng Shui: An ancient Chinese practice of arranging the environment to promote harmony, balance, and positive energy flow by considering spatial arrangement, orientation, and other factors.

Frontal Cortex (Prefrontal Cortex): The part of the brain responsible for executive functions, decision-making, planning, and impulse control.

Functional Magnetic Resonance Imaging (fMRI): A neuroimaging technique that measures brain activity by detecting changes in blood flow and oxygenation levels. fMRI enables researchers to observe which areas of the brain are activated during specific tasks or stimuli, providing insights into brain function and connectivity. It is commonly used in cognitive neuroscience, psychology, and medical research to study various brain processes, such as perception, memory, emotion, and decision-making.

Gamma-Aminobutyric Acid (GABA): A neurotransmitter that inhibits or reduces neuronal activity, promoting relaxation and reducing anxiety.

Gi: In the Korean martial arts tradition, particularly in disciplines like Taekwondo, Gi (also spelled Ki or Qi) refers to the concept of internal energy or life force. Similar to the Chinese concept of Qi or the Japanese concept of Ki, Gi is believed to flow through the body, influencing physical strength, mental focus, and spiritual wellbeing. Practitioners seek to cultivate and harness Gi through training, meditation, and breath control to enhance their martial arts techniques and overall health.

Glutamate: The primary excitatory neurotransmitter in the brain, involved in learning, memory, and synaptic plasticity.

Hanbang: Traditional Korean medicine, emphasising holistic health principles, herbal remedies, acupuncture, and dietary therapy, rooted in Confucianism, Taoism, and Korean shamanism.

Herbal medicine: The use of plants or plant extracts for medicinal purposes, including treating illnesses, promoting healing, and supporting overall health and wellbeing.

Hippocampus: A region of the brain involved in learning, memory consolidation, and spatial navigation.

Holistic: Pertaining to the whole person, considering physical, mental, emotional, social, and spiritual aspects of health and wellbeing.

Homeostasis: The physiological process by which living organisms maintain internal stability and balance in response to changes in the external environment. Homeostasis involves the regulation of various bodily parameters, such as body temperature, blood pressure, pH levels, and fluid balance, within narrow ranges to support optimal functioning and health. This dynamic equilibrium is achieved through feedback mechanisms that detect deviations from set points and activate compensatory responses to restore stability, ensuring the body's internal environment remains relatively constant despite external fluctuations.

Hormones: Chemical messengers secreted by endocrine glands into the bloodstream to regulate various physiological processes and maintain homeostasis in the body. Hormones travel throughout the body, binding to specific target cells or organs, where they exert their effects by influencing gene expression, metabolism, growth, development, and behaviour. Key hormones include insulin, oestrogen, testosterone, adrenaline, cortisol, and thyroid hormones, among others. Imbalances in hormone levels can lead to various health conditions and disorders.

Hypothalamic-Pituitary-Adrenal (HPA) Axis: A complex neuro-endocrine system involved in the regulation of stress response and various physiological processes. The HPA axis consists of the hypothalamus, pituitary gland, and adrenal glands, which work together to produce and release hormones such as corticotropin-releasing hormone (CRH), adrenocorticotropic hormone (ACTH), and cortisol in response to stressors. Activation of the HPA axis triggers a cascade of hormonal reactions that influence metabolism, immune function, mood, and other bodily functions to help the body adapt to stress and maintain homeostasis.

Hypothalamus: A brain region involved in regulating basic biological functions, including hunger, thirst, body temperature, and sleep

Insulin: A peptide hormone produced by the pancreas, specifically by beta cells in the islets of Langerhans (see below), that plays a central role in regulating blood glucose levels. Insulin facilitates the uptake of glucose from the bloodstream into cells, where it is used for energy production or stored as glycogen or fat. Insulin also regulates carbohydrate, lipid, and protein metabolism and is essential for maintaining normal blood sugar levels.

Islets of Langerhans: Clusters of endocrine cells scattered throughout the pancreas, responsible for producing and secreting hormones that regulate blood sugar levels. The islets contain several types of cells, including alpha cells that produce glucagon, beta cells that produce insulin, delta cells that produce somatostatin, and PP cells that produce pancreatic polypeptide. These hormones play critical roles in glucose metabolism and maintaining overall metabolic balance in the body.

Karate: A traditional Japanese martial art emphasising striking techniques using punches, kicks, knee strikes, and open-handed techniques. Practitioners aim to develop physical strength, mental discipline, and self-defence skills.

Ketones: Another class of organic compounds found in some Essential Oils, characterised by the presence of a carbonyl group (C=O) bonded to two carbon atoms within the molecule. Ketones have diverse effects in Aromatherapy, ranging from mucolytic and expectorant to sedative and calming properties.

Ki: In Japanese culture, the equivalent of Chi or Qi, representing the life force or energy that flows through all living things, influencing health, vitality, and wellbeing.

Kirlian Photography: A photographic technique that captures the coronal discharge, or aura, of an object or living organism. Named after Semyon Kirlian, who pioneered the method in the 1930s, it involves placing the subject on a photographic plate and applying a high-voltage, high-frequency electrical field to create an image of the subject's electromagnetic field. Kirlian photography is often used in alternative medicine and paranormal research to visualise energy fields and diagnose health conditions.

Kung Fu: An umbrella term encompassing various Chinese martial arts disciplines characterised by fluid movements, striking techniques, and defensive manoeuvres. Kung Fu emphasises physical fitness, self-discipline, and mental focus, often practiced as a form of self-defence, physical exercise, or cultural expression.

Limbs: In yoga philosophy, the physical postures or exercises (asanas) practiced to promote flexibility, strength, and balance, typically accompanied by breathing techniques (pranayama) and meditation.

Limbic System: A group of brain structures, including the amygdala, hippocampus, and hypothalamus, involved in emotion, motivation, and memory.

Mantra: A sacred word, phrase, or sound repeated silently or aloud during meditation or spiritual practice to focus the mind, cultivate awareness, and invoke specific qualities or energies.

Meditation: A practice of mindfulness, concentration, or contemplation aimed at cultivating inner peace, clarity, and self-awareness, often involving focused attention on breath, sensations, or mental objects.

Meridians: In Traditional Chinese Medicine, the pathways or channels through which Chi (vital energy) flows in the body, connecting various organs and tissues and influencing overall health and wellbeing.

Metabolism: The set of biochemical processes that occur within an organism to maintain life, including the conversion of food into energy (catabolism) and the synthesis of molecules necessary for cellular function (anabolism). Metabolism involves various pathways and enzymes that regulate the breakdown of nutrients such as carbohydrates, fats, and proteins to produce energy and facilitate growth, repair, and other physiological functions. Factors such as age, genetics, diet, and physical activity influence metabolic rate, which affects energy expenditure and body composition.

Mind-Body Connection: The relationship between physical health and mental or emotional wellbeing, emphasising the interconnectedness of mind and body.

Mindcare: A holistic approach to emotion and mental wellbeing that encompasses self-care practices, mindfulness techniques, and emotional regulation strategies aimed at promoting inner balance, resilience, and psychological health. Mindcare emphasises the importance of nurturing one's mental health through activities such as meditation, journaling, stress management, and self-reflection, with the goal of cultivating inner peace and emotional resilience.

Mindfulness: A mental state characterised by present-moment awareness, non-judgmental observation, and acceptance of thoughts, feelings and sensations as they arise, often cultivated through meditation and other practices.

Monoterpenes: A type of terpene found in many Essential Oils, characterised by their molecular structure consisting of two isoprene units. Monoterpenes are known for their antimicrobial, antiviral, and anti-inflammatory properties in Aromatherapy.

Moxibustion: A Traditional Chinese Medicine technique involving the burning of dried mugwort (moxa) near specific acupuncture points or meridians to stimulate circulation, promote healing, and alleviate various health conditions.

Mudra: Hand gestures or symbolic gestures used in yoga, meditation, and spiritual practices to channel energy, express specific concepts, or evoke psychological states.

Naturopathy: A system of alternative medicine that emphasises natural remedies, such as herbal medicine, nutrition, and lifestyle changes, to promote healing and prevent illness.

Neuroplasticity: The brain's ability to reorganise and adapt by forming new neural connections and pathways in response to learning, experience, and environmental changes throughout life.

Neurotransmitters: Chemical substances that transmit signals between nerve cells (neurons) in the brain and nervous system, influencing various physiological and psychological functions, including mood, behaviour, and cognition.

Norepinephrine (Noradrenaline): A neurotransmitter and hormone involved in the body's stress response, promoting alertness and arousal.

Oestrogen: A group of steroid hormones primarily produced in the ovaries (in females) and in smaller amounts in the testes (in males) and adrenal glands. Oestrogen plays a critical role in the development and functioning of the female reproductive system, including the menstrual cycle, ovulation, and pregnancy. It also influences various physiological processes beyond reproduction, such as bone health, cardiovascular function, and cognitive function.

Olfactory: Relating to the sense of smell or the olfactory system, which is responsible for detecting and processing odours. The olfactory system involves specialised cells in the nasal cavity that detect airborne molecules and transmit signals to the brain for interpretation. Olfactory perception plays a crucial role in various physiological and psychological processes, including food detection, environmental awareness, emotional responses, and memory formation. Dysfunction in the olfactory system can lead to anosmia (loss of smell) or hyposmia (reduced sense of smell), affecting an individual's quality of life and overall wellbeing.

Patch test: A method used to assess skin sensitivity to Essential Oils by applying a small amount of diluted oil to a small area of skin and observing for any adverse reactions before widespread use.

Physiology: The branch of biology that studies the normal functions and activities of living organisms and their parts, including bodily systems, organs, tissues, and cells. Physiology explores how these components work together to maintain homeostasis, regulate internal processes, and respond to environmental stimuli, providing insights into biological mechanisms underlying health and disease.

Phytochemicals: Bioactive compounds naturally occurring in plants, including those found in Essential Oils, with health-promoting effects when inhaled or absorbed through the skin.

Pitta: In Ayurveda, one of three Doshas or constitutional types, representing the energy of transformation and metabolism, associated with qualities of fire and water, and influencing digestion, metabolism, and body temperature.

Prefrontal Cortex: See Frontal Cortex.

Prana: In Hindu philosophy and yoga, the vital life force or energy that permeates the universe and sustains all living beings, influencing physical, mental, and spiritual wellbeing.

Pranayama: Yogic breathing techniques aimed at regulating and controlling the breath to enhance vitality, relaxation, and mental focus, often practiced in conjunction with yoga postures (asanas) and meditation.

Psychology: The scientific study of the mind and behaviour, encompassing various aspects of cognition, emotion, perception, personality, development, and social interactions. Psychology seeks to understand mental processes and behaviours through empirical research, observation, and analysis, aiming to enhance wellbeing and address psychological disorders.

Qi: (See Chi).

Qi Gong (Chi Kung): A Chinese system of energy cultivation involving coordinated body movements, breath control, and mental focus to promote physical health, mental clarity, and spiritual growth.

Reiki: A Japanese healing technique based on the channeling of universal life force energy to promote relaxation, stress reduction, and physical and emotional healing through touch or non-touch methods.

Resilience: The ability to adapt and bounce back from adversity, trauma, or stress, maintaining mental and emotional wellbeing.

Schizophrenia: Chronic and severe mental disorder characterised by disturbances in perception, thought processes, emotions, and behaviour, often involving hallucinations, delusions, and impaired social functioning.

Seasonal Affective Disorder (SAD): A type of depression that occurs seasonally, typically during the winter months, due to reduced exposure to sunlight, characterised by symptoms such as low mood, fatigue, and changes in sleep and appetite.

Self-Care: The practice of taking deliberate actions to maintain or improve physical, mental, and emotional wellbeing, including activities such as exercise, relaxation, healthy eating, and seeking professional support when needed.

Self-Compassion: Treating oneself with kindness, understanding, and acceptance, especially during times of difficulty or failure, promoting emotional resilience and wellbeing.

Serotonin: A neurotransmitter involved in regulating mood, appetite, sleep, and social behaviour, influencing feelings of wellbeing and happiness.

Shiatsu: A Japanese form of bodywork or massage therapy based on the application of pressure to specific points on the body to promote relaxation, relieve tension, and restore balance to the body's energy flow.

Social: Relating to or involving interactions, relationships, and connections between individuals, groups, or communities that influence mental wellbeing and social functioning.

Spirituality: A broad concept encompassing personal beliefs, values, practices, and experiences related to the transcendent or divine, often involving a sense of connection to something greater than oneself.

Stoicism: An ancient Greek philosophy emphasising self-control, resilience, and acceptance of fate in the face of adversity, promoting inner peace, emotional stability, and ethical living.

Stress: The body's response to perceived threats or demands, resulting in physiological and psychological reactions that can impact physical health, mental wellbeing, and overall functioning.

Stress Management: Techniques and strategies aimed at reducing or coping with stress, promoting relaxation, and enhancing overall wellbeing.

Substance Use Disorder: A mental health condition characterised by problematic patterns of substance use, leading to significant impairment or distress, including dependence, tolerance, withdrawal, and negative consequences on various life domains.

Synergy: The interaction between different Essential Oils or aromatic compounds that enhances their combined therapeutic effects when used together.

Taekwondo: A Korean martial art focusing on powerful kicking techniques, dynamic movements, and mental discipline. It emphasises self-defence, physical fitness, and personal development through forms and sparring matches.

Tai Chi (Taiji): A Chinese martial art and moving meditation practice characterised by slow, flowing movements, deep breathing, and mental focus to cultivate Chi (vital energy), balance, and inner peace.

Taoism (Daoism): An ancient Chinese philosophical and spiritual tradition centred on the concept of the Tao, or the natural order of the universe, emphasising simplicity, spontaneity, and harmony with nature.

Terpenes: A large and diverse class of organic compounds produced by plants, including Essential Oils. Terpenes contribute to the scent and flavour of Essential Oils and have various therapeutic effects in Aromatherapy.

Testosterone: A steroid hormone primarily produced in the testes (in males) and in smaller amounts in the ovaries and adrenal glands (in females). Testosterone is the primary male sex hormone and plays a key role in the development and maintenance of male reproductive tissues, including the testes and prostate, as well as secondary sexual characteristics such as muscle mass, bone density, and facial and body hair. In females, testosterone contributes to libido, bone health, and muscle strength.

Thalamic Activity: Refers to the electrical and biochemical processes occurring within the thalamus, a structure located deep within the brain that acts as a relay station for sensory and motor signals. Thalamic activity plays a critical role in regulating consciousness, sensory perception, and motor control by transmitting sensory information to the cerebral cortex and coordinating neural pathways involved in sensory processing, attention, and arousal. Dysfunction in thalamic activity can lead to various neurological conditions, including sensory processing disorders, sleep disturbances, and altered states of consciousness.

Thyroid Hormones: Thyroid hormones, including thyroxine (T4) and triiodothyronine (T3), are produced by the thyroid gland and play a central role in regulating metabolism, growth, and development throughout the body. These hormones influence virtually every physiological process, including energy production, heart rate, body temperature, digestion, and brain function. Thyroid hormones are essential for maintaining overall health and wellbeing, and imbalances can lead to various disorders such as hypothyroidism and hyperthyroidism.

Traditional Chinese Medicine (TCM): A holistic system of medicine originating in ancient China, encompassing various practices such as acupuncture, Aromatherapy, herbal medicine, cupping therapy, and dietary therapy. TCM emphasises the balance of Chi (vital energy) and the harmonious functioning of the body's organs to promote health and treat illness.

Vata: In Ayurveda, one of three Doshas or constitutional types, representing the energy of movement and air, associated with qualities of dryness, lightness, and creativity, and influencing bodily functions such as mobility, circulation, and communication.

Ventromedial Prefrontal Cortex (vmPFC): A region of the prefrontal cortex involved in decision-making, emotional regulation, and social behaviour.

Volatile organic compounds (VOCs): Organic chemicals that vaporise easily into the air at room temperature, including some compounds found in Essential Oils that contribute to their aroma and therapeutic properties.

Western medicine: The conventional system of medicine based on scientific principles, biomedical research, and evidence-based practices aimed at diagnosing, treating, and preventing diseases and disorders through medical interventions, pharmaceuticals, and surgery.

Wellbeing: A state of physical, mental, and emotional health characterised by overall satisfaction with life, positive emotions, resilience, and the ability to cope with stress and adversity.

Wellness Coaching: A practice that involves helping individuals set and achieve goals related to physical, mental, or emotional wellbeing, providing guidance, support, and accountability.

Yin and Yang: In Chinese philosophy, the complementary and interconnected forces or principles representing opposing yet interdependent aspects of the universe, such as light and dark, hot and cold, active and passive and female and male, symbolising harmony and balance.

Yoga: A holistic system of physical, mental, and spiritual practices originating in ancient India, including physical postures (Asanas), breath control (Pranayama), meditation, and ethical principles, aimed at promoting health, wellbeing, and self-realisation.

Zen Buddhism: A Japanese school of Mahayana Buddhism emphasising meditation (Zazen), mindfulness, and direct insight into the nature of reality to achieve enlightenment or spiritual awakening.

Printed in Great Britain
by Amazon